FOUNDATIONS OF MODERN ECONOMICS SERIES

Otto Eckstein, *Editor*

PETER B. KENEN *Columbia University*

RAYMOND LUBITZ *Columbia University*

International

Economics

THIRD EDITION

PRENTICE-HALL, INC. *Englewood Cliffs, New Jersey*

13-472613-8

JUL 1 2 '78

Library of Congress Catalog Number 71-135021

PRENTICE-HALL FOUNDATIONS
OF MODERN ECONOMICS SERIES

Otto Eckstein, *Editor*

Current printing (last digit):
10 9 8 7 6 5

PRENTICE-HALL INTERNATIONAL INC., *London*
PRENTICE-HALL OF AUSTRALIA, PTY., LTD., *Sydney*
PRENTICE-HALL OF CANADA, LTD., *Toronto*
PRENTICE-HALL OF INDIA PVT. LIMITED, *New Delhi*
PRENTICE-HALL OF JAPAN, INC., *Tokyo*

Foundations

of Modern Economics Series

Economics has grown so rapidly in recent years, it has increased so much in scope and depth, and the new dominance of the empirical approach has so transformed its character, that no one book can do it justice today. To fill this need, the Foundations of Modern Economics Series was conceived. The Series, brief books written by leading specialists, reflects the structure, content, and key scientific and policy issues of each field. Used in combination, the Series provides the material for the basic one-year college course. The analytical core of economics is presented in *Prices and Markets* and *National Income Analysis,* which are basic to the various fields of application. *The Price System* is a more sophisticated alternative introduction to microeconomics. Two books in the Series, *Evolution of Modern Economics* and *Economic Development: Past and Present*, can be read without prerequisite and can serve as an introduction to the subject.

For the third editions, the books have been thoroughly revised and updated. Topics that have come into the forefront of attention have been added or expanded. To preserve the virtues of brevity, older material has been weeded out. A new book has been added to the Series, *Managerial Economics*, by Farrar and Meyer, designed to show more fully how economic reasoning can be applied to decisions in the business firm.

The Foundations approach enables an instructor to devise his own course curriculum rather than to follow the format of the traditional textbook. Once analytical principles have been mastered, many sequences of topics can be arranged and specific areas can be explored at length. An instructor not interested in a complete survey course can omit some books and concentrate on a detailed study of a few fields. One-semester courses stressing either macro- or micro-economics can be readily devised. The Instructors Guide to the Series indicates the variety of ways the books in the Series can be used.

This Series is an experiment in teaching. The continued positive response has encouraged us to continue to develop this new approach. The thoughtful reaction and classroom reports from teachers have helped us once more in preparing the third editions. The Series is used both as a substitute for the basic textbook and as supplementary reading in elementary and intermediate courses.

The books do not offer settled conclusions. They introduce the central problems of each field and indicate how economic analysis enables the reader to think more intelligently about them, in order to make him a more thoughtful citizen and to encourage him to pursue the subject further.

Otto Eckstein, *Editor*

Contents

International Economics

The Nation

as an Economic Unit

CHAPTER ONE

FOREIGN AND DOMESTIC TRANSACTIONS

The study of foreign trade and finance is among the oldest specialties within economic inquiry. It was conceived in the sixteenth century, a lusty child of Europe's passion for Spanish gold, and grew to maturity in the turbulent years that witnessed the articulation of modern nation-states. In the eighteenth and nineteenth centuries it attracted the very best economists, including Adam Smith, David Ricardo, and John Stuart Mill, whose work supplied the legacy of insights and concepts that have endured to guide the economists of even our own era. (It is interesting to note that Mill furnished the first full formulation of the "law of supply and demand" while trying to explain price determination in international markets, and that, similarly, a large part of modern monetary theory emerged from early efforts to show how foreign trade can affect the level of domestic prices.)

International economics flourishes today because the facts and problems that brought it into being still compel our urgent attention. First, economic conditions and institutions are more uniform within countries. Second, foreign transactions are specially encumbered by public policy. These two points are easy to illustrate.

Language, law and custom rarely differ much within a single country. This internal uniformity makes for easy movement of labor, capital, and enterprise. The tax system is also homogeneous within a country, but differs very markedly from one country to the next. True, the tax systems of our 50 separate states differ quite widely. But the national tax system helps to average out regional differences. Further-

1

more, federal spending tends increasingly to overlay local variations in the quality and quantity of public services.

Internal monetary differences are smallest of all. An elaborate network of markets connects financial institutions within the United States. Funds can flow from region to region, and borrowers can raise cash where it is cheapest, whittling down regional differences in credit conditions. Finally and most important, a single currency is used throughout the country. A five-dollar bill issued by the Federal Reserve Bank of Richmond circulates freely across the United States; it must be accepted everywhere. For that matter, you can cash a check wherever you are known, even if you write the check on a bank hundreds of miles away. How much more complicated life would be if merchants refused to accept currency or checks from other Federal Reserve Districts! You would have to scan every dollar bill, weed out those from other Districts, and swap them for local money at your bank; you would also have to carry a large quantity of cash while traveling and would have to trade one kind for another when crossing state lines.

Goods flow freely among our 50 states. In fact, the American Constitution expressly forbids local interference with interstate commerce. The authors of the Constitution believed that free trade among the states would help cement their fragile political union. For similar reasons France, Italy, Germany, the Netherlands, Belgium, and Luxembourg have forged a Common Market in Western Europe as the first step toward a political confederation; they permit a free flow of goods inside Western Europe and impose a common tariff on goods from outside. But trade between countries is ordinarily burdened with customs tariffs that work to raise the prices of imported goods; and countries have sometimes used more formidable barriers—quotas that restrict the quantity of imports or the freedom to buy foreign currency. The United States puts quotas on foreign petroleum and on each of a dozen farm products. The quotas on imported oil protect the domestic oil industry; those on farm products are meant to deny foreign farmers the benefits provided by our high price supports for farm products. These tariffs and quantitative barriers are doubly restrictive. First, they raise the prices of foreign goods and handicap those goods in competition with domestic products. Second, they impose a heavy workload on the would-be importer. Look at the fragment from the U.S. tariff schedule reproduced in Fig. 1–1, and try to compute the rate of duty on a shockproof, self-winding watch, 1 inch wide, with 16 jewels.

Differences between monetary systems may have an even greater adverse impact on foreign trade than tariffs and quotas. Almost all international transactions involve two or more moneys. An American wholesaler importing French champagne has first to determine its price in French francs, then the price of the franc in U.S. dollars—the franc-dollar *exchange rate*. He must order the champagne, buy French francs with dollars, then pay over the francs to the French exporter. He thereby incurs extra cost and runs extra risks. The costs are the commissions charged by specialized dealers in foreign exchange. The risks arise because exchange rates can change. Most governments are pledged to maintain

Schedule 7-2-E(716.30-719)
Watch movements, assembled, without dials or hands, or with dials or hands whether or not assembled thereon:

Having over 7, but not over 17 jewels:

Not over 0.6 inch in width	$1.80 each + 9¢ for each jewel over jewel 7
Over 0.6 but not over 0.8 inch in width	$1.35 each + 9¢ for each jewel over 7
Over 0.8 but not over 0.9 inch in width	$1.35 each + 9¢ for each jewel over 7
Over 0.9 but not over 1.0 inch in width	$1.20 each + 9¢ for each jewel over 7
Over 1.0 but not over 1.2 inch in width	.90 each + 9¢ for each jewel over 7
Over 1.2 but not over 1.5 inch in width	.90 each + 9¢ for each jewel over 7
Over 1.5 but not over 1.77 inch in width	.90 each + 9¢ for each jewel over 7
Adjusted, but not self-winding (and if a self-winding device cannot be incorporated therein), and not constructed or designed to operate for a period of 47 hours without rewinding	base rate + 50¢ for each adjustment
Self-winding (or a self-winding device can be incorporated therein), or constructed or designed to operate for a period of 47 hours without rewinding, but not adjusted	base rate + 50¢ each
Adjusted and self-winding (or if a self-winding device can be incorporated therein), or constructed or designed to operate for a period of 47 hours without rewinding, but not adjusted	base rate + 50¢ each + 50¢ for each adjustment

FIG. 1—1 A fragment of the U.S. tariff schedule. The tariff on a single watch must be calculated by adding up several separate rates: the basic rate (based on width and jewels), the extra duty on adjustments, the duty on each jewel, and the special duty on self-winding mechanisms.

their exchange rates at or near fixed points called *parities*. Currently, for example, you can buy a French franc for 18 cents, or 5.55 French francs for a dollar. But governments allow exchange rates to vary by as much as 2 per cent of parity in response to changes in supply and demand, and sometimes make changes in the parities themselves. In 1956, the French franc was *devalued* (made cheaper in terms of other currencies), going from 3.50 per dollar to 4.20 per dollar; in 1958, it was devalued again, from 4.20 to 4.94 per dollar; a third devaluation, in 1969, brought the price to 5.55 per dollar. Sterling has been devalued twice in the postwar period. In 1947, the pound went from 4.80 dollars to the pound to 2.80; in 1967, it went to 2.40 dollars per pound. In 1961, by contrast, the German mark and Dutch guilder were made to *appreciate* (made more expensive in terms of other currencies) and, in 1969, the mark was again made to appreciate. Day-to-day changes in exchange rates can cut into traders' profits, and sudden changes in the parities can turn profits into losses. The American importer of French champagne could lose heavily if the price of the franc were to rise on the foreign exchange market after he had signed his sales contract but before he had bought his francs.[1]

Foreign investors have also to cope with foreign-exchange problems, and these may be more complex than those faced by traders, for investors have a longer time-horizon. They likewise face difficult tax problems, as tax laws and tax rates differ radically from one country to the next.

PERSPECTIVES AND CRITERIA

The international economist views the world as a community of separate nations, each with its own constellation of natural resources, capital, knowledge, and manpower, its own social and economic institutions, and its own economic policies. He usually assumes that transport costs are negligible and that most markets are purely competitive. He often assumes that labor and capital are perfectly mobile within each country, but not free to move from one country to the next.

Using these assumptions, he seeks to explain international flows of goods, services, and capital, to assess their impact on domestic welfare, and to forecast their response to changes in national policies. He concentrates on policies expressly designed to affect foreign trade and payments—those involving tariffs, exchange rates, and the taxation of foreign-source income. But he must also look at other policies—at tax rates, public spending, monetary management, labor legislation, and the rest—since they prescribe the terms on which international transactions take place.

The international economist will sometimes study trade and payments from the standpoint of a single country, but is just as likely to adopt a cosmopolitan perspective and seek to ascertain their impact on the world as a whole. When taking a single country's viewpoint, he is apt to begin his analysis by pretending that the country in question was at first isolated from the outside world, but then began to trade with other countries. When taking the cosmopolitan viewpoint, he is likely to start out by pretending that there were at first no differences in policies or barriers to trade among its several regions, but that those regions then became separate nations, each with its own institutions and policies. The perspectives and assumptions he employs in his analysis may greatly affect his conclusions, especially those that pertain to the selection of national policies.

Whatever his particular perspective, however, the international economist is chiefly concerned with individuals. Like other economists, he is an intellectual

---

[1]Traders and investors can sometimes protect themselves against exchange-rate changes by buying or selling foreign currency on the *forward* foreign-exchange market. There, they can arrange to swap dollars for francs three months from now, at a price (exchange rate) fixed today. Doing so, however, they merely transform risk into cost, for forward foreign exchange may be more expensive than *spot* (current) foreign exchange.

descendant of Adam Smith and of the nineteenth-century Utilitarians, and though he may for analytical purposes treat the nation as a single unit, he is not likely to regard it as the end in view. Instead, he appraises any change in public policy by the same criteria his confrères employ in other specialties. He says that such a change is potentially good if the individuals who gain by the change could compensate the individuals who lose. He would probably go on to say that if the losers have smaller incomes than the gainers, the compensation should be performed. Furthermore, the international economist uses the same tests of economic performance that guide other specialists.

First, he is concerned with *efficiency:* How do international trade and payments affect the allocation of resources within a country? How do they redistribute economic tasks among the participating countries?

Second, he is concerned with *equity:* How does trade alter the distribution of income and wealth within a country? How does it redistribute income and wealth among countries?

Third, he is concerned with *stability:* How does trade affect a country's reaction to domestic disturbances and its freedom to deal with domestic problems? Does it, perhaps, "import" extra instability through its external transactions?

Fourth, he is concerned with *economic growth:* Does a country's foreign trade affect its growth rate? Should the less-developed countries gear their new production to foreign markets, making their way as exporters, or should they draw back from foreign trade to seek greater self-sufficiency?

Do not be deceived by the abstract formulation of these questions. The search for answers is propelled by the daily needs of business and government, not by scientific curiosity alone. The problems posed by foreign trade, investment, and aid, and by international monetary relations, impinge on a host of issues confronting the United States. After a century of intensive exploitation, its endowment of raw materials is dwindling. Should it cut back its domestic output of ores and oil to rely instead on cheaper foreign sources, or should it protect its domestic producers against import competition to encourage further exploration and exploitation? How can the United States act to improve the distribution of the world's food supplies? Can it reconcile its own farm policies with those of other exporting countries like Canada and, simultaneously, with those of key importers like Britain and India? Should our tax policies be changed in response to the surge of private American investment abroad—the building of factories in Europe to manufacture goods that were formerly exported from the United States? How will this migration of capital and enterprise affect economic life here and abroad?

How can the United States maintain an over-all balance in its international transactions, given its commitments to foster economic growth at home and also to defend and develop friendly foreign countries? Is the special role of the U.S. dollar as an international currency beneficial, or burdensome? If beneficial, how can it be strengthened? If burdensome, how can the international monetary system be altered without damaging the network of trade and payments built up so patiently since the Second World War? How best can the United States and other countries aid the new nations of Asia, Africa, and Latin America, and how will these young countries fit into world trade once they have begun to modernize their own economies?

We shall not try to survey this whole range of issues in the hundred pages at our disposal, but will try to illustrate the methods and perspectives employed by economists as *they* seek to answer them. In Chapters 2 and 3 we will ask how international trade and investment affect the allocation of world resources, and how the various barriers modify that allocation; we will glance at the diplomacy of tariff policy; and we will take a quick tour of the European Common Market. In Chapters 4 and 5 we will take up the *balance of payments* and the foreign-exchange market; we will study equilibrium, displacement, and adjustment in international payments; and we will survey the roles of gold and the U.S. dollar in the international monetary system. Finally, in Chapter 6, we will examine foreign trade and investment as "engines" of economic growth, seeking to determine how they can contribute to the development of the new nations.

CHAPTER TWO

THE BASIS FOR TRADE
AND GAINS FROM TRADE

Differences in prices are the basic cause of trade and reflect international differences in costs. But why should costs differ from country to country? How can Japan produce cameras, sewing machines, and cotton shirts more cheaply than the United States? Many people would reply that Japan has lower costs because it has lower wages, and wages are important costs. This explanation seems plausible enough; it is firmly based on fact. But it is not adequate.

If wage rates were decisive for cost differences and trade, Japan would undersell the United States in every product line and every market. Yet Japan imports machinery and cotton from the United States, and other low-wage countries buy American goods in great variety and enormous quantities. As a matter of fact, the United States sells more to other countries than it buys abroad, despite its high wages. Differences in wage rates, then, cannot explain trade patterns, and one must look elsewhere for the basis of trade.

An enduring two-way flow of goods must be traced to systematic international differences in the *structure* of costs and prices: some things must be cheaper to produce at home and will be exported to other countries; some things must be cheaper to produce abroad and will be imported from other countries. This generalization is basic to the theory of foreign trade, and is known as the *principle of comparative advantage*. Stated most precisely, it asserts that a country will export the products it can produce at the lowest *relative* cost. Japan, it contends, can export cameras and textiles because it can produce those goods with the least

7

sacrifice of alternative production. The United States can export machinery and cotton because it can produce those goods with the smallest sacrifice. Cameras may cost less than machines in both countries, but the cost difference is far from uniform, thus creating opportunities for profitable trade.

The Sources of Comparative Advantage

A nation's comparative advantage and trade pattern are heavily affected by its resource endowment—both natural and man-made. Nature has decreed important and enduring differences between countries. Some of them are rich in copper, others in petroleum; some have huge waterfalls, others have fertile plains. Some countries have just enough rainfall for rice or cotton cultivation, whereas some have too much, and others have next to none. Furthermore, some countries have the resource *combinations* required for the performance of certain vital tasks: one may have the plains *and* rainfall needed to grow wheat; another may have a rich deposit of iron ore *next to* a waterway that can carry ore to coal. Finally, some countries have populations large enough to man and support great, complex industries, but others are so underpopulated that their land cannot even be worked nor their ores extracted.

In one sense, people are a natural resource; in another, they are a major man-made resource. Mere numbers are the gift of nature. But the skills and attitudes of a population are the work of man and strongly influence a country's comparative advantage. A nation rich in people but poor in skills may be suited to certain tasks, but not to the production and export of manufactured goods. A nation that has very few persons per square mile but has lavished its energies on technical training is likely to enjoy a comparative advantage in the production of precision goods.

Going one step further, we must distinguish between types of skill. Some nations have large numbers of factory workers adept at handling modern machinery. Others have an abundance of engineers and scientists and specialize in new, research-laden products. It has been said, for example, that the United States enjoys a comparative advantage in research and innovation, but that it loses out to its competitors as each of its new products ages, the market for it grows, and the knowledge required to manufacture it is diffused among other countries. The United States, it is argued, has always to race ahead in technology merely to stand still in world markets.

One part of a nation's capital stock is embodied in its labor force as agricultural, industrial, and scientific skill. Another part is embodied in physical equipment: roads, airports, harbors, and dams; trucks, aircraft, ships, and turbines; factories and office buildings; tractors, lathes, conveyors, and typewriters. These represent the portion of past output that was reserved for investment rather than consumption.

Notice that natural and man-made resources can interact powerfully. Bauxite was not valued as a natural resource until the development of the elec-

8

trolytic process for extracting aluminum, and of the cheap electric power required to fuel that process. Aluminum itself was not very valuable until the metalworking industries found ways to use it. Pitchblende was a geological curiosity until man's skill and malevolence found a use for uranium, and ways to separate one isotope from others. Population also interacts with technology. Modern mass-production methods need mass markets and are apt to take root first in regions of dense settlement that provide outlets for large lots of standardized products. In consequence, such regions are apt to enjoy a comparative advantage in the export of mass-produced articles, and they may well retain their advantage *vis-à-vis* regions that start later or on a smaller scale. Notice, too, that comparative advantage always has a time dimension. It depends on the state of technology at a given moment and on its subsequent diffusion. It also depends on the history of capital accumulation and, therefore, on the rate of economic growth.

A Simple Model

To show how a difference in resource endowments can call forth foreign trade, consider two countries, America and Britain, which are identical in all ways but one. Both of them have 120 man-days of labor available. Both use 2 man-days of labor to grow a ton of potatoes and have enough arable land to employ all their workers in potato-farming. But America's coal deposits are very near to the surface and only 1 man-day of labor is required to dig out a ton, whereas Britain's deposits are much farther down and 4 man-days of labor are required to dig out a ton. If its whole labor force were employed growing potatoes, America could produce 60 tons per day; 2 man-days of labor can grow a single ton and 120 man-days of labor are available. If, instead, the whole labor force were employed digging coal, America could produce 120 tons per day; 1 man-day of labor can dig out a single ton and 120 man-days are available. If, finally, America wished to produce some potatoes and some coal, it could secure any one of several combinations. To produce a single ton of coal, it would have to divert 1 man-day of labor from its potato fields, reducing potato output by half a ton. To produce 2 tons of coal, it would have to divert 2 man-days from the potato fields, reducing potato output by 1 ton.

America's *production possibilities* are summarized by the line AB in Fig. 2–1. The distance OA measures the output of coal that would be obtained if the entire labor force worked in the coal mines (120 tons); the distance OB measures the output of potatoes that would be obtained if the entire labor force worked in the potato fields (60 tons). Points along the line AB describe the combinations of coal and potatoes that could be produced simultaneously. At point P, for example, America would be producing Oc coal and Od potatoes. It would obtain Oc coal by foregoing Bd potatoes.

If Americans were not allowed to trade with outsiders, their pattern of consumption would have to coincide with one of the coal and potato combinations lying on AB. The output mix prevailing at a particular time would, of course,

9

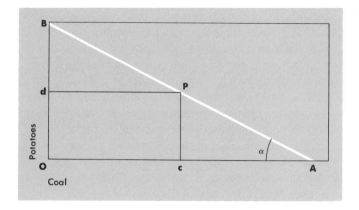

FIG. 2–1 American production possibilities. The line AB shows how many tons of potatoes America can grow for a given level of coal production. If America produced Oc tons of coal, it could grow Od tons of potatoes. The steepness of AB (measured by angle a) gives the price of coal in terms of potatoes.

depend on consumer preferences—demand conditions—and on the price of coal in terms of potatoes. That price ratio, in turn, would be given by the comparative labor costs of coal and potato production. Labor is the only variable input (factor of production) used in this very simple economy, and a single man-day of labor can mine a whole ton of coal but can grow only half a ton of potatoes. A ton of coal will therefore cost a single man-day's wage, whereas a ton of potatoes will cost 2 man-days' wages. A ton of coal will be half as expensive as a ton of potatoes, and it will exchange for half a ton of potatoes in America's markets.[1] This same price relationship appears in Fig. 2–1; it is represented by the slope (steepness) of *AB*, the production possibilities frontier. The distance *OB* is half the distance *OA*, indicating that a ton of coal will sell for half a ton of potatoes.

Britain also needs 2 man-days of labor to produce a ton of potatoes, and consequently could grow 60 tons if it used all its labor in its potato patches. But it needs 4 man-days of labor to dig out a ton of coal, and could mine only 30 tons if it used all its labor in its coal mines. By implication, Britain could produce a single ton of coal by diverting 4 man-days of labor from potato-growing, thereby giving up 2 tons of potatoes. Britain's production possibilities are described by the line *A'B'* in Fig. 2–2. Maximum potato output, *OB'*, is the same as

---

[1]One can arrive at this same result by examining *marginal* costs. If product markets are perfectly competitive, prices must equal marginal costs. If labor is the only variable input and labor requirements are constant for all output levels, marginal costs must equal labor requirements per unit of extra output multiplied by the wage rate. Hence:

$$\text{Price of Coal} = \text{Marginal Cost of Coal} = \text{Wage Rate} \times \text{Man-days of Labor Needed to Produce a Ton of Coal}$$
$$\text{Price of Potatoes} = \text{Marginal Cost of Potatoes} = \text{Wage Rate} \times \text{Man-days of Labor Needed to Produce a Ton of Potatoes}$$

Therefore:

$$\frac{\text{Price of Coal}}{\text{Price of Potatoes}} = \frac{\text{Man-days Needed to Produce a Ton of Coal}}{\text{Man-days Needed to Produce a Ton of Potatoes}}$$

The wage rate cancels out in this calculation, for it must be the same in both industries.

in America, because the two countries are endowed with the same amounts of labor and are equally efficient in potato-growing. But maximum coal output OA', is smaller in Britain than in America, for Britain's coal lies somewhat deeper in the ground.

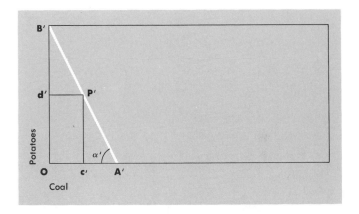

FIG. 2–2 British production possibilities. The line $A'B'$ shows how many tons of potatoes Britain can grow for a given level of coal production. The steepness of $A'B'$ (measured by angle a') gives the price of coal in terms of potatoes. Britain can produce as many potatoes as America (OB' equals OB in Fig. 2–1), but far less coal.

The line $A'B'$ in Fig. 2–2 is much steeper than the line AB in Fig. 2–1. This difference is explained by the difference in mining costs and implies a difference in relative prices. British coal must be twice as expensive as British potatoes, for labor costs are twice as high. Isolated from the outside world, Britain would produce and consume some combination of coal and potatoes lying on $A'B'$, and a ton of coal would be worth 2 tons of potatoes.

But now allow America and Britain to trade, and suppose that goods can move between them without transport costs. The opportunity for trade will create a single Anglo-American market and, therefore, a single price for coal in terms of potatoes. This new common price will lie between the national extremes—less than the prior British price (2 tons of potatoes per ton of coal) and higher than the prior American price (half a ton of potatoes per ton of coal). Britain can now obtain a ton of coal without surrendering as many potatoes as it had to sacrifice to furnish its own coal. It will tend to specialize in potato-growing and will use its potatoes to buy American coal. America is able to obtain more potatoes for its coal. It will tend to specialize in coal-mining and to use its coal to buy British potatoes.

To illustrate this rearrangement of production, suppose that the new Anglo-American coal price is stabilized at 1 ton of potatoes per ton of coal. Britain can now import a ton of coal by growing and exporting a single ton of potatoes. Without trade, by contrast, it had to sacrifice 2 tons of potatoes to produce a ton of coal. In effect, Britain saves 2 man-days of labor on each ton of coal consumed. For its part, America can import a ton of potatoes by mining and exporting a

11

single ton of coal. Without trade, it had to sacrifice 2 tons of coal to produce a ton of potatoes. America saves 1 man-day of labor on each ton of potatoes consumed.

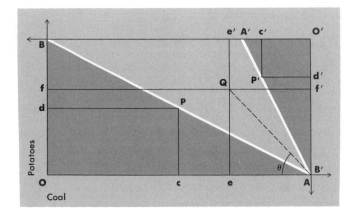

FIG. 2–3 Trade between America and Britain. Before trade, America produced Oc coal and Od potatoes. Britain produced O'c' coal and O'd' potatoes, and each country consumed all it produced. When trade is opened, America produces OA coal and no potatoes; Britain produces O'B' potatoes and no coal. America consumes Oe coal and exports eA coal to buy British potatoes; Britain consumes O'f' potatoes and exports f'B' potatoes to buy American coal. America can then consume Of potatoes (Of being equal to f'B' British exports); Britain can consume O'e' coal (O'e' being equal to eA American exports). Each country can consume more of both products than it did before trade. The price of coal, shown by the θ, is higher than the pretrade British price (the slope of A'B').

To explain why the common price might settle at 1 ton of potatoes per ton of coal we must also consider demand conditions. At each possible common price, we can ascertain Britain's supply of potatoes and demand for coal and America's supply of coal and demand for potatoes. If the price of coal were too high, the supply of coal would be greater than the demand and the demand for potatoes greater than the supply. The price of coal would have to fall. At the equilibrium price, the Anglo-American market will exactly clear; the demand and supply for both products will each be equal.

Fig. 2–3 restates our results with greater generality. There, the left-hand triangle, OAB, is the American production-possibilities frontier, just as it appeared in Fig. 2–1. The right-hand triangle $O'A'B'$ is Britain's production-possibilities frontier, taken from Fig. 2–2 but flipped upside-down. If America and Britain could not trade, each would be confined to its own frontier, America at P and Britain at P'. When they are allowed to trade, they can rearrange production and consumption to mutual advantage. America can specialize in coal-mining, using all its labor to produce OA tons. Britain can specialize in potato-farming, using all its labor to produce $O'B'$ tons. America can then consume Oe tons of coal and export eA tons to pay for potatoes. Britain can consume $O'f'$ tons of potatoes and export $f'B'$ tons to pay for coal. America can buy Of tons of potatoes (equal to the *f'B'* Britain will export), and Britain can buy *O'e'* tons of coal (equal to the *eA* tons America will export). American consumption can move from *P* to *Q*, and British consumption can move from *P'* to *Q*. Each country can consume more of both goods than it did before trade.[2]

Figure 2–3 describes two ways to view the gains from trade. First, it shows that every country can escape the confines of its own resource endowment. Before trade, each country had to consume a combination of coal and potatoes lying on its own production-possibilities frontier. Its choice was restricted by its resource endowment. But trade allows every country to reshuffle output and to consume a combination of commodities it could never produce by itself. In consequence, the individual consumer enjoys a wider range of choice. Fig. 2–3 also shows that trade enlarges global output by allowing every country to specialize in the tasks it does best. Before trade, total coal output was *Oc plus c'O'*. With trade, it rises to *OA* (an increase of *ce plus e'c'*). Before trade, total potato output was *Od plus d'O'*. With trade, it rises to *O'B'* (an increase of *df plus f'd'*). This increase in output was required for each country to increase its consumption of both commodities in the fashion described by Fig. 2–3. It also leads to a basic proposition in international economics: *Free trade is the best regime for the world as a whole.* The increase in coal and potato output shown by Fig. 2–3 is the largest increase possible. Hence, free trade allocates economic tasks to maximize world output and income.

Productivity, Wages, and Prices

Figure 2–3 describes the free-trade price of coal as the slope (steepness) of the dotted line *AQ*. This line is steeper than *AB*, but flatter than *A'B'*. Coal has become more expensive in America, but cheaper than it was in Britain. But we have not been shown how this price comes into being, save to mention the interaction of supply and demand. To study this important process, we must take a look at wage rates, absolute prices, and exchange rates.

Suppose that the American wage rate stands at $15 per man-day, while the British wage rate stands at £5. At the opening of trade, a ton of American potatoes will cost $30 (2 man-days are needed to grow a ton), and a ton of coal will cost $15 (1 man-day is needed to mine a ton). A ton of British potatoes will cost £10 (2 man-days are needed to grow a ton), and a ton of coal will cost £20 (4 man-days are needed to mine a ton).

Suppose, further, that the exchange rate between the dollar and the pound

---

[2]The point Q could settle down anywhere within the unshaded part of the diagram, depending on demand conditions. It could also settle on AB or A'B', where the new common price would be at one of the national extremes. In that case one country would capture all the gains from trade, but the other would be no worse off than it was without trade. If the price came to rest on A'B', the old British level, America would specialize completely and garner all the gains from trade; it would get its potatoes more cheaply than it could at home. Britain would tend to specialize in potatoes, but would also mine coal. If the price came to rest at AB, the old American level, Britain would specialize completely and garner all the gains from trade; it would get its coal more cheaply than it would at home. America would tend to specialize in coal but also grow potatoes.

13

has been fixed by international agreement at $3 per pound. The dollar price of British potatoes will be $30 per ton; the dollar price of British coal will be $60 per ton. Neither country will have reason to import potatoes, for the dollar prices are the same. But Britain will import American coal, since British coal costs $60 a ton whereas American coal costs $15 a ton. At the agreed exchange rate, the British wage rate is too high compared to the American; British comparative advantage in potatoes does not show through.

If both countries' work forces are fully employed before trade began, the advent of trade will cause an excess demand for labor in America because of the British demand for American coal. It will also cause unemployment in Britain because of the shift in British demand from domestic to foreign coal. In consequence, wage rates will rise in America and fall in Britain. This change in wages, however, will make British potatoes cheaper than American, whether priced in dollars or pounds, and both countries' consumers will start to buy potatoes in Britain. British farmers will plant larger crops, taking up the labor released from Britain's coal mines; American farmers will cut back their crops, releasing labor to America's mines.

This process will not cease until unemployment disappears in the British coal mines and the labor shortage ends in America's coal mines. And these things will not happen until consumers rearrange their purchases in response to the price changes resulting from the wage-rate change. When, finally, those wage changes have ceased, the price of American coal will be higher than it was to start (because of the increase in American wages), while the price of British potatoes will be lower than it was to start (because of the decrease in British wages). The wage-rate changes will have offset America's higher productivity, allowing Britain's comparative advantage in potato-growing to show through as a lower price.[3]

Some Evidence

Statistical studies of trade and productivity show that the principle of comparative advantage can explain actual patterns of trade, despite the existence of tariffs and other trade barriers. Differences in wage rates serve to offset over-all differences in national efficiency. Trade flows are consequently governed by differences in relative internal costs, reflecting variations in comparative efficiency from one domestic industry to the next.

A British economist, Sir Donald MacDougall, has compared British and American exports prior to the Second World War, looking at 24 separate industries. His results are summarized in Section A of Table 2–1. In every case, American output per worker was higher than British output per worker. But it was 5.4

[3]This same process of adjustment could have been accomplished by changing the exchange rate. Suppose that money wage rates were absolutely rigid in Britain and America but that the exchange rate connecting their currencies was free to fluctuate in response to changes in supply and demand. The British demand for American coal would then be manifest in a demand for American dollars that would drive up the price of the dollar expressed in terms of pounds. This increase in the price of the dollar would lower the cost of British potatoes expressed in dollars and would raise the cost of American coal expressed in pounds. Americans would start to buy British potatoes.

times as high in the production of electric-light bulbs and only 1.1 times as high in the production of cement. Average American wage rates, by contrast, were about twice as high as average British wage rates. Whenever, then, American workers were less than twice as efficient as their British competitors, British goods could compete with American goods in world markets; British exports were larger than American exports. When, instead, American productivity was more than twice as high as British productivity, the corresponding U.S. industry had the cost advantage, and in 7 out of 12 such cases, American exports were larger than British exports.

These results show up again in the post-war period. An American economist, Robert Stern, has reworked MacDougall's example using trade and labor data for 1950. At that time, U.S. wage rates were about three times as high as British wage rates. When U.S. labor productivity was more than three times British productivity, then, American exports were usually larger than British exports. Stern has also studied a larger sample comprising 39 manufacturing industries. In 15 of these 39 cases, U.S. labor was more than three times as efficient as British labor, offsetting the British wage-rate advantage, and in 11 of these 15 cases, U.S. exports were larger than British exports. In the other 24 cases, U.S. productivity was higher than British, but not as much as three times as high. In 21 of these 24 cases, British exports were larger than American exports. Stern's results are summarized in Table 2–1. Section B gives 1950 data for the same 24 industries studied by MacDougall; Section C gives 1950 data for Stern's larger sample.

Table 2–1 OUTPUT PER WORKER AND TRANSATLANTIC EXPORTS, GREAT BRITAIN AND THE UNITED STATES

Difference in Labor Productivity	Number of Industries		
	Total	In Which U.S. Exports Larger than British	In Which U.S. Exports Smaller than British
A. Pre-war trade (24 industries): U.S. wages double British wages			
U.S. output per worker more than double British	12	7	5
U.S. output per worker not more than double British	12	0	12
B. Post-war trade (24 industries): U.S. wages treble British wages			
U.S. output per worker more than treble British	7	5	2
U.S. output per worker not more than treble British	17	2	15
C. Post-war trade (39 industries): U.S. wages treble British wages			
U.S. output per worker more than treble British	15	11	4
U.S. output per worker not more than treble British	24	3	21

Source: Robert M. Stern, "British and American Productivity and Comparative Costs in International Trade," Oxford Economic Papers, Vol. 14, No. 3 (October, 1962), pp. 278, 288.

These uniformities are striking indeed. The number of exceptions is very small, especially in Stern's 39-industry sample. One would, in fact, expect many more exceptions. Most countries impose barriers to foreign trade that interfere with the principle of comparative advantage. Furthermore, each of the product classes studied includes a great number of separate commodities, and one must allow for differences in quality. Finally, labor is not the only factor of production, so that labor productivity is not the only cause of trade. If high U.S. output per worker were entirely due to the more intensive use of machinery, the U.S. advantage in efficiency would be partly offset by higher payments for the use and maintenance of that machinery.

A Two-Factor Model

The two-country, two-product, labor-cost model used thus far in this chapter is much like the model developed by Ricardo early in the nineteenth century. Multi-country, multi-commodity versions of that model came into use toward the end of the century and were employed to show that the chief conclusions drawn from Ricardo's work are readily susceptible of generalization. They also supplied a framework for statistical studies of the type conducted by MacDougall, Stern, and others. This family of labor-cost models can serve a great number of important purposes—to identify the gains from foreign trade and to describe the cost-price adjustments required to capture the gains from trade through international specialization. But labor-cost models shed much less light on several other aspects of foreign trade: the influence of differences in factor supplies on international specialization, the impact of economic growth on trade patterns, and the impact of trade on national economies. To study these additional issues, we require more elaborate theoretical models incorporating several factors of production: land, labor, and capital.

The multi-factor model we shall use is derived from the work of two Swedish economists, Eli Heckscher and Bertil Ohlin. The model assumes constant returns to scale (a given percentage increase in all inputs will generate the same percentage increase in output), takes no account of transport costs, and assumes that tastes are the same everywhere. Unlike the labor-cost model, it goes on to assume that each country has access to the same technology, and would employ the same methods of production if confronted with identical factor prices. It thereby rules out the differences in relative efficiency that served as the basis for foreign trade in the labor-cost model we studied before.

The Heckscher-Ohlin or *factor-endowments* approach to trade theory proceeds from two suppositions:

1. Products differ in factor requirements—cars require more machine-time (capital) per worker than, say, cotton cloth or furniture, and aircraft require more machine-time than either cars or cotton cloth.[4]

[4]One could, of course, make cars by several methods, differing in capital-intensities. One could use a small machine-shop or an automated plant. One could also weave cloth by many methods, some of them quite highly mechanized. The choice of technique will depend on the prices of the factors of production—the wage rates paid to workers and the rental prices of machinery (the interest costs of capital and allowances for repair and depreciation). But the factor-endowments model assumes that the product which is most capital-intensive at one set of factor prices is also most capital-intensive at every other set.

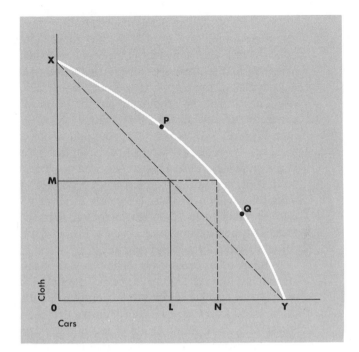

FIG. 2–4 Production-possibility frontier with variable techniques. When cloth output falls by one-half, from OX to OM, car output will rise to ON, not OL which is one-half of OY. The price of cars in terms of cloth is given by the slope of XPQY. When car production rises and cloth production falls, as in the shift from P to Q, the price of cars in terms of cloth rises.

2. Countries differ in factor endowments—some have large amounts of capital per worker (the capital-abundant countries) and some have very little (the labor-abundant countries).

The theory then argues that capital-abundant countries will tend to specialize in capital-intensive goods such as cars and aircraft, and will export some of their specialties in order to import labor-intensive goods. Similarly, labor-abundant countries will specialize in labor-intensive goods and will export their own specialties in order to import capital-intensive goods. To put the proposition in general terms: *Trade will be based on differences in factor endowments and will serve to relieve each country's factor shortages.*

We shall illustrate this proposition with a production-possibilities frontier based on the use of two factors of production—labor and machinery—to produce two products—cars and cloth. This new frontier, *XPQY* in Fig. 2–4, describes the different combinations of cars and cloth a particular economy can produce. The slope of the frontier indicates the amount of car production that must be sacrificed to produce an additional yard of cloth. In consequence, this slope measures the price of cars in terms of cloth. The slope steepens as we move along *XPQY* from, say, *P* to *Q*, indicating that an increase in car production will raise the relative price of cars. In this case of *increasing costs*, as opposed to the *constant costs* of the Ricardian example, the cost of producing cars increases as more cars are produced.

17

Why does a two-factor model produce this result? It is tempting to argue that if we started at X on $XPQY$ and reduced cloth production by one-half, half of all the machines and labor in the economy would be shifted into car production. With constant returns to scale, car production would be OL, equal to one-half of OY, and cloth production would be one-half of OX, or OM. Generalizing, one might argue that the production-possibilities frontier should be the straight line connecting X and Y. On $XPQY$, however, a 50 per cent reduction in cloth is quite correctly shown to permit a car output of ON, greater than OL. Recall our earlier assumption that products differ in factor requirements. Hence an increase in car production and a decrease in cloth production do not shift the two factors of production in equal proportions. A 50 per cent cut in cloth production allows more than OL of car output because an efficient economy will rearrange factor use according to the different factor requirements of the products. Table 2–2 presents a numerical example that will help explain this point and allow us to derive some important propositions.

Suppose an economy is endowed with a capital stock of 10,000 machines and a labor force of 8,000 man-years. The upper and lower sections of Table 2–2 compare two points on its production-possibilities frontier, listing the quantities of the two factors used in each industry and the outputs those factors produce. In each situation, the total use of machines and labor adds up to the same total factor endowment. When cloth output falls by 50 per cent, from 1 million yards to 500,000 yards, that industry does not release machine and labor in equal 50 per cent amounts. Machine use falls by more that 50 per cent (from 4,000 to 1,000), and labor use falls by less than 50 per cent (from 5,000 to 3,000). The economy might have produced 500,000 yards of cloth by cutting factor use in equal proportions, but then the factors released to the car industry would not have produced as many additional cars. It is more efficient to release more machines and less labor from the labor-intensive cloth industry to the machine-intensive car industry.

Table 2–2 OUTPUT MIXES AND FACTOR INPUTS

	Cloth	Cars	Total Factors Used
Output	1 million yards	100,000 cars	
Inputs:			
Machines (number)	4,000	6,000	10,000
Labor (man-years)	5,000	3,000	8,000
Machines per man-year	0.8	2.0	
Output	500,000 yards	250,000 cars	
Inputs:			
Machines (number)	1,000	9,000	10,000
Labor (man-years)	3,000	5,000	8,000
Machines per man-year	.33	1.6	

Factor Prices and Output

In Table 2–2, the machine intensity of car technology is shown by a machine–labor ratio that is greater in the car industry than in the cloth industry for each output mix. The table also reveals that when car production increases, the machine–labor ratio falls in *both* industries. With a fixed total-factor endowment, an increase in the output of the machine-intensive product requires that both products be produced in a less machine-intensive way. Both industries must economize on the use of machinery when output switches to the machine-intensive product. How is this result accomplished? The answer, as one might expect, is a change in the prices of machines and labor. An increase in car production raises the demand for machines relative to the demand for labor because of the greater machine-intensity of car production. The increased demand for machines raises the price of machines relative to the price of labor, inducing producers to substitute labor for machinery in both industries.

We can now see why cars become more costly relative to cloth as car output rises. The machine-intensive car industry must use a less favorable (more labor-intensive) factor ratio, whereas the labor-intensive cloth industry may use a more favorable (more labor-intensive) factor ratio. Putting the point differently, the increase in the rental price of machines relative to the wage of labor will raise the price of cars relative to the price of cloth because cars require more machines per worker. In terms of Fig. 2–4, a move from P to Q will pull resources out of cloth and increase the relative demand for machinery, thereby raising the price of machines and of the machine-intensive product. Our model uncovers an important link between factor prices and product prices. When the price of cars rises, the price of machines also rises; when the price of cloth rises the price of labor rises. The price of a factor rises with the rise in the price of the product that requires its intensive use.

Factor Endowments and Trade

Consider two countries—a labor-abundant country called Manymen and a capital-abundant country called Fewmen. The factor endowments of the two countries will determine the position and shapes of their production-possiblities frontiers. In Fig. 2–5 Manymen's frontier MM' shows a bias towards the production of cloth, the labor-intensive product; and Fewmen's frontier, FF', towards the production of cars. At any given output mix, for example, along the rays OTS or OLR, where both countries produce cars and cloth in the same proportions, Fewmen produces cars relatively more cheaply; compare the slopes of the frontiers at S and T or R and L. Fewmen has a higher capital–labor ratio than Manymen and will always produce a given output mix using more capital-intensive methods. Because of Fewmen's greater capital abundance, the relative price of capital will be lower and the relative price of cars, the capital-intensive product, will also be lower than in Manymen. Fewmen, with abundant capital, will produce cars at each output mix more cheaply than Manymen. A difference in

19

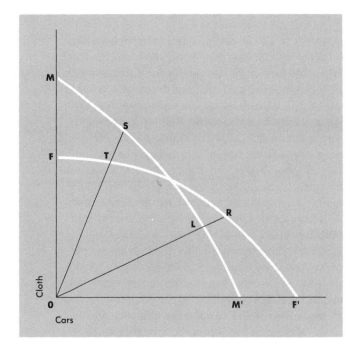

FIG. 2–5 The effect of factor endowments on the production-possibility frontier. MM', Manymen's frontier, shows a bias towards the production of cloth, the labor-intensive good; FF', Fewmen's frontier, shows a bias towards the production of cars, the capital-intensive good. At the output mixes shown by the rays OTS and OLR, the slopes at S and L on MM' are steeper than at T and R on FF'. Cars are more expensive to produce in Manymen.

factor endowments creates a difference in relative product prices and, given identical demand conditions, establishes the basis for trade.

Before trade begins Manymen will be at A and Fewman at B in Fig. 2–6. Cars are cheap and cloth is dear in Fewmen whereas in Manymen cars are dear and cloth is cheap.[5] Both countries are confined to their production-possibility frontiers. Trade, when opened, will take place at an international price determined by demand and supply conditions given here by the slope of the line GTE. Manymen will produce at G and consume at T, while Fewmen will produce at E and consume at T. Manymen produces SG cloth, keeps for its own consumption SR, and exports GR. It produces CR of cars, consumes CT, and imports the difference, RT. It exchanges GR of cars for RT of cloth at the international price ratio. Fewmen imports TQ of cloth (equal to Manymen's exports, RG) to bring its car consumption to T, and it pays for these imports with QE of car exports (which equals Manymen's imports, RT). The international market clears at the price ratio GTE.

Each country increases the output of the good intensive in its abundant factor: Fewmen produces more cars and Manymen more cloth. Thus, trade enables both countries to specialize in the product intensive in its abundant factor

[5] If the citizens of Manymen had a very strong taste for cloth or those of Fewmen for cars, it is conceivable that demand differences could offset endowment differences in determining pretrade prices. However, the assumption of identical tastes rules out this possibility.

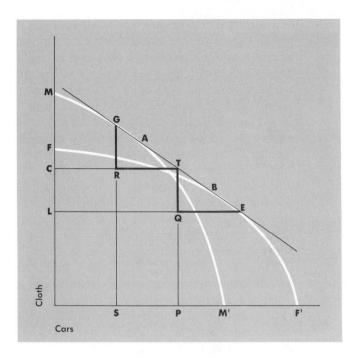

FIG. 2–6 Trade between Manymen and Fewmen. Before trade, Manymen produces and consumes at A and Fewmen at B. Trade will take place at the international price given by the slope of GTE. Manymen will produce at G and consume at T. It produces SG cloth, consumes SR and exports RG; it produces CR cars, imports RT and consumes CT. Fewmen produces LE cars, consumes LQ and exports QE; it produces PQ cloth, imports TQ to bring its consumption to PT. Fewmen's export of QE cars equals Manymen's imports (RT), and its imports of TQ cloth equals Manymen's exports (RG).

and import the product intensive in its scarce factor. This leads to an increase in global economic welfare because T lies outside both production-possibility frontiers, and both countries have a larger set of goods available to them. Trade allows a country to escape from the confines of its factor endowments by trading for goods that use factors that are scarce at home.

Unlike the Ricardian case, specialization is not complete; each country continues to produce some of each product. Relative prices and costs after trade are the same for Manymen and Fewmen. International trade under increasing costs raises the cost of producing cars in Fewmen, as more cars and less cloth are produced, and lowers the cost of producing cars in Manymen as more cloth and fewer cars are produced. As the comparative cost model leads us to expect, trade will take place up to the point at which the relative costs of production are equalized.

Trade and Factor Prices

The equalization of product prices brought about by trade leads to an intriguing corollary: *Free trade will tend to equalize factor prices across the participating countries.* To illustrate this proposition, consider Manymen and Fewmen again. Manymen's labor abundance causes production to be labor-intensive throughout the economy before the opening of trade, and means that wages will

21

be low compared to the rental prices of machines. In Fewmen, by contrast, wages will be high compared to rental prices. If the two countries can trade with each other, Manymen can relieve its shortage of machines by importing the capital-intensive product (cars), and its wages will rise relative to rental rates. Fewmen can likewise relieve its shortage of labor by importing the labor-intensive product (cloth), and its wages will fall relative to rental rates.

This is what free trade will do. As wages would be relatively high in Fewmen before trade began, cloth would be expensive compared to cars. With the opening of trade, Fewmen will therefore export cars and import cloth. To do so, it will increase its car production and cut back its cloth production. These shifts in the pattern of production will, in turn, augment Fewmen's demand for machines and will reduce its demand for labor. Manymen, by contrast, will increase its cloth production and cut back its car production, and these shifts will augment its demand for labor and will reduce its demand for machines. If there are no transport costs between the two countries, free trade will equalize product prices in Fewmen and Manymen. It will thereby equalize the two countries' factor prices.

In actual practice, of course, factor prices are *not* equal around the world —and the differences are far too great to be explained by transport costs and trade barriers. Hence, the simple model we have been developing cannot be perfectly applicable to the real world; it may ignore important economies of scale, and the fact that modern technology is not available to every country. Yet the *tendency* described by the Heckscher-Ohlin model—the *reduction* of factor-price differences through trade—may still be quite important.[6]

Suppose, again, that cars and cloth cannot move between the countries. Wages would be higher in Fewmen than Manymen, and if there were no travel costs, workers would migrate from Manymen to Fewmen. If, further, this migration were to continue for as long as wage rates differed, it would render the two countries very much alike. Fewmen would wind up with as many machines and very much more labor than it had to start with, but the *ratio* of man-years to machines would be exactly equalized in the two countries. This is because the wage-rate difference causing migration would persist for as long as the ratio of man-years to machines were lower in Fewmen than in Manymen. It would only vanish when the ratios were equalized.

This example suggests one more way to look at the gains from trade. It argues that free trade can sometimes substitute for international movements of labor and capital. Factor movements and free trade each serve to reduce differences in factor prices. Factor movements do so by erasing differences in national factor endowments. Free trade does so by offsetting those differences. Trade

[6]Furthermore, available statistics may exaggerate international differences in factor prices. When we compare wage rates around the world, we are comparing rather different things. Some countries' wage statistics are heavily weighted with large returns to skill; others' are dominated by the lower wages of unskilled labor. If one were to compare the wage rates of equally skilled workers, of equally fine land, and so on, being sure to match like with like, factor prices might prove to be more nearly equal than they usually appear.

eliminates the need for a redistribution of productive factors by reallocating economic tasks. It allows every country to make the best use of its own factor endowment.

THE USE
AND ABUSE OF TARIFFS

All the models you have seen illustrate the same basic proposition: *Free trade maximizes world output.* Furthermore, those models show that free trade is beneficial to all of the participating countries. Each country can escape the confines of its own resource endowment to consume a collection of commodities better than the best it can produce.

Why, then, do we still hear so much clamor for protective tariffs and other trade barriers? The answer to this question has two parts. Many fallacious arguments against foreign trade are easily refuted but have a peculiar immunity to logic. Economists can demolish the protectionists' argument, but speeches about "cheap foreign labor" and the "imperatives of national defense" have enormous popular appeal. Furthermore, several of the arguments for tariffs survive rigorous analysis. Free trade may be best for the world as a whole, but it may not be best from a single country's standpoint: tariffs and other trade barriers may sometimes be employed to redistribute the gains from trade in favor of one country, to redistribute income within a single country, to stimulate domestic employment, or to facilitate economic development.

The Hardy Fallacies

Every now and then, someone tells you that the United States must use tariffs to protect itself from cheap foreign labor. He is armed with lots of figures about low foreign wages, and his numbers are usually accurate. But his inference is totally wrong. In fact, you encountered the answer to his argument when you learned how trading prices are determined. The very first example in this chapter started by assuming that British and American wage rates were exactly equal before the opening of trade. British wages were £5 a day and the exchange rate stood as $3 per pound, so that British and American wages worked out at $15 a day. But when trade was opened, excess demand raised the American wage, and unemployment reduced the British wage. This result was not a caprice of the market; it served a necessary function. If British wages had not fallen, British potato prices would not have declined, and Britain could not have sold potatoes in order to import American coal. The change in wage rates offset Britain's lower productivity and was vital to the process of adjustment that attends the opening of trade. The "cheap foreign labor" argument for tariffs neglects this important link between wages and efficiency. It regards a systematic wage-rate difference as an unfair competitive handicap when, in truth, the difference is required for trade

23

to take place. Wage-rate difference between countries serves to translate comparative advantage into price, and prices guide the flow of trade.

Other protectionists argue for tariffs in the interests of national security—to protect domestic industries capable of turning out guns and planes when war breaks out. This may be the oldest argument in the protectionists' arsenal, and it must be admitted that it did make sense some time ago when, without its own steel mills, no nation could in fact make guns or planes if cut off from its peacetime suppliers abroad. But the national-defense argument for tariffs makes much less sense today. In the thermonuclear age, a nation's ability to protect itself no longer depends upon its capacity to mobilize civilian industries for arms production. A nation cannot count on having time for the process of conversion—and might not have much industry left to convert after a nuclear attack. In today's world, the weaponry on hand at the outbreak of a major war is apt to be decisive and the peacetime protection of defense-related industries is anachronistic.

One must, of course, contemplate the possibility of "limited" wars, like those in Korea and Vietnam. But such wars are not likely to isolate the United States or other major countries from critical materials and finished manufactures. If, indeed, such a conflict were sufficiently widespread to jeopardize normal sources of supply, it could hardly be contained or fought with conventional weapons, but would "escalate" quite rapidly.

Note, finally, that the burdens of national defense ought to be apportioned equitably, whereas tariffs levied to protect critical industries tax the peacetime users of specific products by raising the prices of competitive imports. If, then, an industry must be supported in the interests of national security, it should be subsidized directly, out of the government's general tax revenues.

Tariffs and the Distribution of the Gains from Trade

But what of the "respectable" arguments for tariffs—those that appeal to national gain and survive the economist's rigorous scrutiny? One such argument asserts that a single country can extract larger gains from trade by imposing tariffs on goods from abroad. This resembles the familiar proposition that a monopolist can increase his profits by limiting his sales. By restricting imports with a tax, a country *can* sometimes force down the price at which other countries sell to it, and thus improve its *terms of trade*. If it carries the process too far, the loss it suffers by foregoing the consumption of imported products will exceed the gain it takes by reducing foreign prices. The monopolist faces an analogous danger: if he cuts back his output too severely, he will lose more on volume than he gains on price. The fact remains, however: a country that enjoys a strategic position in world trade can rearrange the gains from trade in its own favor by a judicious use of import restrictions.

Figure 2–7 depicts trade in cloth between Manymen and Fewmen before the imposition of the tariff. As in an ordinary supply-and-demand diagram, the price of cloth is measured on the vertical axis and the quantity of cloth on the horizontal axis. Part B of the diagram shows that, in the absence of trade, the price of cloth in Fewmen will be at OP_1 determined by the intersection at R_1 of the domestic supply curve, S_d, and the domestic demand curve, D. The quantity pro-

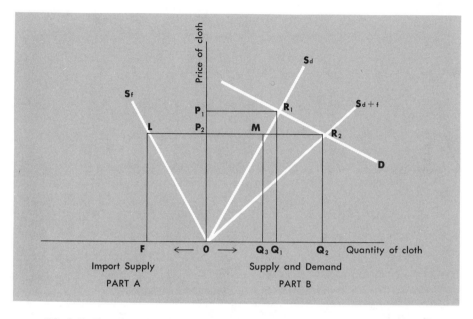

FIG. 2–7 The effect of imports on Fewmen's production and price of cloth. Before trade, the price of cloth is OP_1, and production and consumption are at OQ_1. S_f is the supply curve of imports, which when added to S_d, lowers the price to OP_2. Domestic production falls to OQ_3, but consumption rises to OQ_2 as imports of Q_2Q_3 (equals OF) make up the difference.

duced and consumed is OQ_1. Now allow imports of cloth from Manymen to enter Fewmen. Manymen's export supply curve, S_f in Part A of Fig. 2–7, is added horizontally to Fewmen's S_d supply curve, to generate the aggregate supply curve, S_{d+f}. The horizontal distance between S_d and S_{d+f} equals the distance between the vertical axis and S_f and represents cloth imports. With trade, the new price is OP_2, given by the intersection at R_2 of S_{d+f} and D, and the quantity consumed is OQ_2 or P_2R_2, comprising P_2M of domestic production and MR_2 or LP_2 of foreign production. Trade has lowered the price and increased the quantity consumed.

Now suppose that Fewmen imposes a 30 per cent tariff on cloth imports. Fewmen's citizens are required to pay a price for cloth imports 30 per cent above the price Manymen's exporters receive. Since Manymen's exporters must still receive the same net price for any given quantity supplied, the actual market price in Fewman must be 30 per cent higher for any given quantity. These facts are

25

represented in Fig. 2–8. In Part A of Fig. 2–8, the foreign export supply curve is shifted upward by 30 per cent to S_{f+t} (SB/BG equals 30 per cent of BG). In Part B, the domestic aggregate supply curve is also displaced to S_{d+f+t}. It is now

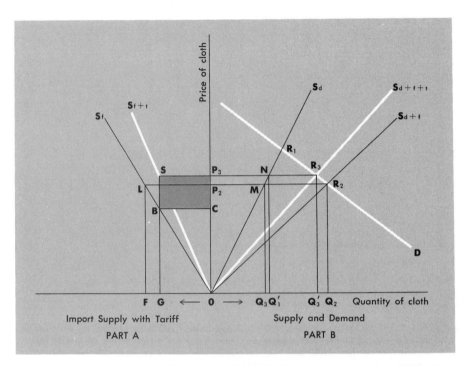

FIG. 2–8 The impact of a tariff. A tariff shifts the foreign supply curve to S_{f+t} and the home-and-import supply curve to S_{d+f+t}. The domestic price rises from OP_2 to OP_3 and imports from Q_2Q_3 to $Q'_1Q'_3$ (equals OG) because of the drop in cloth consumption from OQ_2 to OQ'_3 and increase in domestic cloth production from OQ_3 to OQ'_1.

the sum of S_{f+t} and S_d. The price in Fewmen rises to OP_3 and the quantity consumed falls to OQ'_3 (equal to P_3N of domestic production *plus* NR_3 or SP_3 of foreign production). This tariff on cotton cloth has several effects. Because the price of cloth has risen in Fewmen, there has been a drop in Fewmen's cloth consumption by $Q_2Q'_3$ in Part B. For that same reason, however, there is a new stimulus to local production, and Fewmen's own output has been enlarged by $Q_3Q'_1$ in Part B. Hence, there is a double squeeze on imports from Manymen— a decrease in consumption and an increase in import-competing production, so that imports from Manymen fall by FG in Part A. Finally, Fewmen's government collects CP_3 of tariff on each yard of imported cloth, for a total of CP_3SB, the shaded area in Part A.

To complete the analysis of Fewmen's tariff, we would have to allow for the impact of this new tax revenue on Fewmen's fiscal policies. It could spend this tariff revenue or remit it to the public by lowering some other tax; the final equilibrium position depends on its decision. But let us disregard this last refinement and suppose that the point R_3 locates the exact equilibrium position once the tariff is imposed. Notice that the price paid by Fewmen's citizens is higher than it was under free trade (OP_3 *is higher than* OP_2), but that the price paid to Manymen's exporters is lower than it was under free trade (OC is lower than OP_2). Fewmen is able to obtain its imports more cheaply—at a smaller sacrifice of domestic resources. It has secured better terms of trade.

To generalize, a country can capture a larger share of the gains from trade if the foreign supply curve slopes upward and if the foreigner does not retaliate by imposing tariffs of his own. If the foreign supply curve were horizontal, the supply price of imports would not fall (the terms of trade would not improve). If the foreigner were to retaliate, he might recoup his losses, and leave Fewmen worse off than it was with free trade. Fewmen might then impose another round of tariffs and in the end both countries could lose out, for the global gains from trade would shrink as trade was reduced by each successive round of tariffs. Yet governments have sometimes been tempted to use tariffs to improve their terms of trade, and a free-trade situation may not endure unless it is reinforced by international agreements barring the use of tariffs and other trade controls.

Tariffs and the Distribution of Domestic Income

Tariffs can also be employed to alter the domestic distribution of income. Remember that the product-price differences that give rise to trade have their clear counterparts in factor-price differences. Remember, too, that free trade tends to equalize product prices between the participating countries and, therefore, to equalize those countries' factor prices.

Now let us turn the argument on end. Starting with free trade and equal factor prices in Fewmen and Manymen, let Fewmen impose a tariff on imported cloth. This, you have seen, will raise the price of cloth in Fewmen and lower it in Manymen. It will thereby raise the wage rate in Fewmen and will reduce rental rates on machines. The tariff will encourage Fewmen's cloth production and will discourage its car production, for Fewmen's auto exports will contract with the drop in its cloth imports. In consequence, the tariff will increase Fewmen's demand for labor (the input used intensively in cloth production) and will lower its demand for machines (the input used intensively in car production). It will raise Fewmen's wage rates and reduce Fewmen's rental rates, redistributing income in favor of labor.

Equity versus Efficiency

Thus far, you have seen how tariffs can redistribute income between countries and within them. Trade restrictions, however, are a haphazard way to achieve redistribution. Countries with the market power to affect the terms of trade by imposing tariffs—and the pressure groups that influence domestic legislative processes—are not necessarily deserving of aid through redistribution. More importantly tariffs are an inefficient way to redistribute income. They eat away a part of the pie they are redividing, sacrificing output in the name of equity.

This conclusion follows directly from what you know about free trade. If free trade maximizes global output, any deviation from free trade will reduce world production, leaving less to go around. Figure 2–8 illustrates this point, too. It shows that a tariff replaces low-cost imports with high-cost domestic production. When a tariff is imposed, the last unit of domestic cloth will cost OP_3 dollars to produce (as its price must equal its marginal cost). By contrast, the last unit of import cloth will cost OC dollars (P_3C dollars less). Hence, the substitution of domestic for foreign cloth fostered by a tariff is wasteful of world resources.

Tariffs and Employment

We have tried to show how tariffs can be used to affect the allocation of resources and the distribution of income. They may also be imposed to affect the *utilization* of resources—the levels of employment and production.

When two countries start to trade, they may not strike an equilibrium right away. One country's prices may be higher than the other's when those prices are compared at the prevailing exchange rate, and that country will be compelled to reduce its wage rates. Recall our earliest example of America and Britain. With the British wage rate before trade at £5 and the exchange rate at $3 per pound, the British price of potatoes equaled the American price. To realize its comparative advantage in potatoes Britain had to cut its wage rates. If a country in Britain's position fails to do so, its least efficient industries will shrink, yet its more efficient industries will not grow to take up the slack. The country will trade from a point *inside* its production-possibilities frontier, not from a point *on* that frontier, and free trade may be worse than no trade at all.

If, then, wage rates and other costs are very rigid, a country may gain by restricting its foreign trade. Tariffs will divert demand from foreign to domestic goods, raising domestic output and employment. This result is most likely to occur if the country's unemployed resources are concentrated in its import-competing industries. Tariffs can also combat unemployment caused by a decline in domestic demand during the business cycle, rather than by wage and price disparities revealed at the opening of trade.

Once again, however, tariffs are inefficient policy instruments. They can only stimulate employment by expanding import-competing industries, not the more efficient export industries. Far better, then, to foster wage-rate flexibility or, what may be simpler, to change the exchange rate until a high-cost country's prices are aligned with those of its competitors. Such a country should *devalue* its currency, charging its citizens more for a unit of foreign currency and selling its own currency more cheaply to foreigners. A devaluation raises the domestic price of foreign goods (imports), as foreign currency becomes more expensive. To this extent, it is much like a tariff. But a devaluation also lowers the foreign price of domestic goods (exports), as domestic currency becomes cheaper for foreigners. Unlike a tariff, a devaluation stimulates export industries along with import-competing industries, and does not distort resource allocation.

To put the same point more strongly: tariffs tend to shift one country's unemployment onto its trading partners. One country's import-competing industries (those that benefit from tariff protection) are other countries' export industries (those that make the best use of their resource endowments). Tariffs are a "beggar-my-neighbor" remedy for unemployment.

Tariffs and Economic Transformation

Most of the standard arguments for tariff protection imply a permanent departure from free trade. One group of arguments, however, advocates a *temporary* deviation. From time to time, it is said, a country must make major changes in its product mix. It must reallocate resources in a large way, not just at the margin, and may find it easier to make the change behind the protection of a tariff wall.

There are two versions of this argument for *transitional* protection: one of them promises economies of scale, the other promises economies of age. The first version reminds us that production costs may rise quite steeply for a while, but will begin to fall when output has attained a level that justifies the use of modern machinery and mass-production methods. It consequently recommends that tariffs be imposed to stimulate domestic production and that those tariffs be retained until the growth of internal market has allowed domestic firms to imitate the most efficient methods used in other countries. Once they are "over the hump," it is argued, domestic producers will become fully competitive and may even be able to export, so that they will not need permanent protection, and tariffs can be cut.

The second version of the argument urges protection for an "infant industry," and was given its most famous formulation by Alexander Hamilton in his *Report on Manufactures*. A young industry, it argues, may be less efficient than one that has been long established. It may lack seasoned managers, skilled labor, and reliable suppliers of raw materials. Hence, a young industry may warrant protection until it has matured and cut back its unit costs so as to compete with foreign producers. In effect, this version forecasts that temporary tariffs to young industries will actually expand the production-possibilities frontier, and that world output will then be greater because of the transitional departure from free trade.

Both of these traditional versions of the argument for transitional protection enjoy wide respect. However, the argument needs careful qualification. One must show why an entrepreneur should receive tariff protection, rather than borrow in the capital market to cover his early losses and repay his debts when his firm matures to profitability. Capital is borrowed at an interest rate that should meas-

29

ure the social rate of return on capital—the value of investment to the whole economy. Investment projects that can earn that rate should be undertaken; those that earn less should not be undertaken because they absorb resources that can be better used elsewhere (that have a higher social rate of return). If, then, a firm cannot repay capital borrowed at the social rate of return the investment is not *socially* profitable and it should not qualify for tariff protection.

The case for transitional protection needs restatement. It can be justified only if the capital market functions imperfectly so that the market rate of interest does not reflect the social rate of return on capital. In most economies undergoing large-scale transformation, it is probably true that the capital market (if one exists) is highly imperfect, and the market interest rate, distorted by fragmentation and monopoly elements, will be higher than the social rate of return. In these circumstances, the inability of an investment to earn the market rate of interest does not mean that the investment is socially unjustified. There may be a case for transitional protection.

Further problems must be solved if one is to apply transitional protection correctly. First, one must decide which industries can capture sufficient economies of scale or economies of age to survive after tariffs have been removed. If a country protects all its young industries, it will waste precious resources; almost any industry can grow if given sufficient protection, but some will not endure when their tariffs end. Next, one must determine how large a tariff is required to foster the development of a healthy infant. Too much protection will encourage an excessive expansion, and the protected industries will contract when tariffs are removed. Finally, one must decide if the gains are worth the cost. The use of tariffs, even temporarily, will reduce world output during the transition and may even reduce the real income of the country applying them. These direct and certain losses must be weighed against the distant and uncertain gains offered by protection.

Transitional protection can also pose practical problems. Few industries will readily concede that they have grown up and do not need their tariffs. During their adolescence, moreover, they will have acquired influential spokesmen in government, having become important to the national or regional economy. It will then be difficult to strip them of their tariffs and expose them to the competition they grew up to face. Finally, some governments seem to believe that tariffs can *create* new industries; they restrict imports even when skilled labor, raw materials, and capital are too scarce to allow industrial development.

An additional, analytically valid argument for protection in a newly industrializing nation is based on the assumption that some industries benefit the economy in ways that are not reflected in their own earnings. One firm, for example, may train labor later employed by other firms. These benefits are known as *external economies*. They should be counted when the social return on any investment is measured; and an industry creating external economies, but unable to withstand foreign competition, deserves tariff protection if those external economies outweigh the social cost of the protection. Protection should continue for as long as this situation holds. The external economies argument is subject to misuse, as is the older infant-industries argument. One must decide which industries create external economies large enough to warrant protection, at what rate the protection should be given, and for how long it should endure.

In brief, the occasions that justify transitional protection may be quite rare, and an indiscriminate application of transitional arguments may do great damage. As with most other tariff arguments, there may be better ways to reach an objective—ways that do not sacrifice income or invite retaliation.

SUMMARY

The structure and benefits of foreign trade derive from an uneven distribution of natural and man-made resources. Each country's endowment of land, minerals, skills, and machinery equips it to perform certain tasks more efficiently than others. Free trade allows a country to do the work it can do best, then to trade the products of its most efficient industries for those that other countries make more economically. Trade is based on comparative advantage, not absolute advantage. Adjustments in wage rates (or exchange rates) compensate for differences in over-all efficiency, allowing each country to adapt its production to its own resource endowment. The price system supplies the incentives to efficient specialization, and when wage rates are flexible, can also make the over-all cost-price adjustments needed to offset differences in absolute efficiency.

From the standpoint of the world as a whole, free trade is best. It serves to maximize global output and is, therefore, a substitute for factor movements. A single country, however, may be able to improve its own position by restricting its imports—by using protective tariffs or other trade controls to swing the terms of trade in its favor. But a tariff that is levied to redistribute income will also reduce it, and is that much more harmful to other countries. There are similar objections to the other arguments for protective tariffs—for tariffs to alter the domestic distribution of income and to stimulate employment, and there are serious practical objections to the use of tariffs as catalysts to economic growth in developing countries.

Problems in Trade Policy

CHAPTER THREE

TARIFF THEORY
AND TARIFF HISTORY

At one time or another, every tariff argument has been invoked to justify high import duties, and some of them have been employed by those who advocate free trade. Modern tariff history, then, is also a history of tariff theory, and shows how economic theory can affect policy.

Divergent Tariff Trends: 1815–1860

During the first half of the nineteenth century, the infant-industries argument for tariffs enjoyed a vogue in the United States. The country had just started its industrial development and sought to shelter its young manufacturers from foreign competition. At about that same time, the distributional argument was used in Great Britain with opposite intent: to reduce existing tariffs. Just as the United States was moving toward protection, Great Britain was moving toward free trade.

The United States had taxed its imports from its very birth as a nation. But its early tariffs, though protective in effect, were chiefly designed to raise revenue for the federal government. In those days there was no income tax, and the government relied on excise levies to finance its spending. Tariffs were the most important of those levies. Taxes on imports were very easy to collect; one had merely to police the ports and coastline. It would have been still easier to tax the country's major exports—cotton and tobacco—but the southern states that grew and sold these products had insisted that the Constitution prohibit export duties.

32

They feared that the federal government, dominated by the more populous North, would seek to pay its way by taxing Southern produce.

By 1815, however, there was strong support for a new tariff law fashioned to protect the young manufacturers of New England and the Middle Atlantic states. The Napoleonic Wars had disrupted ordinary channels of trade, and Jefferson's Embargo, designed to prevent the impressment of American seamen by forbidding them to go to sea, had cut this country off from British textiles and hardware. The wars and embargo were equivalent to *prohibitive* tariffs on imported manufactures, giving American industry unrivaled opportunities for growth. But with the coming of peace and resumption of trade, British goods began again to cross the Atlantic, and American manufactures lost ground. Despite the opposition of the South, which naturally preferred to import cheaper foreign products, Congress levied higher duties on woolens and cottons in 1816 and placed higher taxes on imported glass, iron, and cutlery in 1824.

The North–South controversy over tariffs reached a bitter peak after 1828. In that year, the Southerners sought to outmaneuver their antagonists by amending a pending tariff bill. They proposed high duties on raw wool and other crude materials, hoping that the Northern manufacturers who used those materials would reject the entire tariff bill. But the stratagem failed and the bill became law. Its duties were the highest ever imposed prior to the Civil War (see Fig. 3–1), and it was promptly dubbed "The Tariff of Abominations." It inspired South Carolina's "Ordinance of Nullification," which proclaimed a state's right to abrogate federal legislation, asserting that "the tariff law of 1828, and the amendment to the same of 1832, are null and void and no law, nor binding upon this State, its officers and citizens." But this first overt challenge to federal power met firm resistance from President Andrew Jackson, and the furor died down with passage of a compromise tariff in 1833.

In the 1840's the federal budget developed an embarrassing surplus and the Secretary of the Treasury proposed to forego excess tax revenues by reducing tariffs. The average rate of duty on dutiable imports was brought down toward 26 per cent as protective duties were cut sharply in 1846, and again in 1857. But the United States was still out of step with Western Europe, which was moving closer to free trade.

The free-trade movement started in Great Britain as part of a broader assault on the ancient powers of the aristocracy. It sought to end the political hegemony of the rural gentry, who were the chief beneficiaries of the tariffs on imported grain known as the Corn Laws. As in the United States, therefore, tariff policy was entangled in broad constitutional questions, including the issue of parliamentary reform. But the free-trade movement also owed intellectual debts to Adam Smith, who had made an *allocative* case for free trade fully 50 years before the debates on the Corn Laws:

> What is prudence in the conduct of every private family, can scarce be folly in that of a great kingdom. If a foreign country can supply us with a commodity cheaper than we ourselves can make it, better buy it of them with

33

some part of the produce of our own industry, employed in a way in which we have some advantage. The general industry of the country, being always in proportion to the capital which employs it, will not thereby be diminished . . . but only left to find out the way in which it can be employed with the greatest advantage. It is certainly not employed to the greatest advantage, when it is thus directed toward an object which it can buy cheaper than it can make.

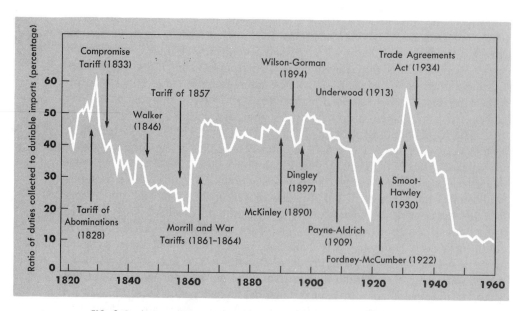

FIG. 3–1 Average U.S. rates on duty on dutiable imports. Legislation raising U.S. duties is usually reflected in an increase in the average on or after passage of the legislation. Legislation cutting U.S. duties is usually reflected in a decline in the average on or after passage. (Source: United States Department of Commerce, Bureau of the Census, *Historical Statistics of the United States* and *Statistical Abstract of the United States, 1961.*)

The free-trade movement was further indebted to David Ricardo and other disciples of Adam Smith who made a *distributive* case against the tax on grain. They contended that the Corn Laws were doubly injurious to the wage-earner. First, tariffs raise food prices, reducing the purchasing power of the worker's wage. Second, tariffs increase land rents at the expense of business profits, and low profits mean less saving, less investment, and therefore less demand for labor.

Britain had actually started toward free trade before the Napoleonic Wars. William Pitt had lowered many duties in 1784, and cut back others two years later in the Eden Treaty with France. After the Napoleonic Wars, the Tory government abolished or reduced many duties on industrial raw materials, responding to appeals by the merchants of London, who had a vital stake in free trade. These reductions were supported by Britain's manufacturers, as tariffs on raw materials raised their production costs. They were not opposed by the gentry, who did not produce the materials involved. But during the next decade, attention turned to the tax on grain—a much more explosive issue. In 1842 the Tory government of Sir Robert Peel successfully defeated a Parliamentary motion to repeal the Corn Laws, taking the side of the gentry. But the Irish potato famine of 1845–1846 forced Peel to allow larger grain imports so as to relieve the food shortage. He suspended the Corn Laws in 1845 and split his own party in 1846 by moving for permanent repeal. The Liberal governments that followed later, led by William Gladstone, completed the task, dismantling most of Britain's other tariffs.

The Triumph and Decline of Free Trade: 1860–1914

In its next step toward free trade, Britain turned from legislation to diplomacy. The Cobden–Chevalier Treaty of 1860 pledged Britain and France to a reciprocal reduction of tariffs, including a reduction in the British tax on French wines. The French then negotiated tariff treaties with other European countries and with the German customs union, or *Zollverein,* organized under Prussian auspices to permit free trade within Germany. The *Zollverein* reduced its external tariffs in exchange for French concessions on German exports.

The commercial treaties of 1860–1870 had two effects. First, they brought about new tariff cuts, enlarging world markets. Second, they *generalized* all of the tariff reductions each country had already made. They included the *most-favored-nation* clause, a standard provision in commercial treaties under which each signatory grants the other every concession given to third countries. Under this clause, France gave the *Zollverein* all of the concessions it had given England in the 1860 treaty. The *Zollverein* was not obliged to make concessions in return, but was committed to grant France the benefits of every tariff cut it had given or would give to any other country.

The free-trade movement, however, was soon to be defeated by a massive and irresistible combination of shifting attitudes and changing circumstances. The 1870's witnessed a sharp change in Europe's colonial policies. Imperialist sentiment had been virtually dormant for half a century, and no major colonies were founded after the Napoleonic Wars, apart from French acquisitions in North Africa. But suddenly the European powers began to scramble for tropical real-estate. The partition of Africa began and was nearly finished in the two decades after 1870. There was renewed rivalry in the Near East and Orient. Bellicose nationalism captured European politics and was soon manifest in measures to protect domestic industry (especially the sectors needed to make armaments) and to obtain control over foreign raw materials.

At about this same time European agriculture experienced a disastrous change of fortune. Railroads and steamships brought wheat from Russia, the United States, and other distant countries into competition with German and French grain. Even Germany, a major exporter, began to import wheat as farm

35

prices fell. During the decades in which they exported grain, European farmers and landowners had favored free trade, just like their counterparts in the American South. But when farm prices fell, the farmers changed their minds, and with this change, the balance of political power swung toward protection. In Germany and France alike, a new coalition of nascent industry and injured agriculture reversed the trend in Europe's tariff policies.

The tide turned first in Germany in 1879. Six years earlier, Bismark had abolished the tariff on iron, and announced that tariffs on iron products would terminate in 1877. But he had over-reached himself, and when the Junkers of the east and farmers of the south united to support the beleaguered manufacturers of the Ruhr and Rhineland, he was forced to backtrack. In 1879, Bismark brought forward a new tariff affording substantial protection to industry and agriculture.

This new turn toward higher tariffs was defended by invoking the infant-industries argument. That argument, indeed, was given its most elaborate formulation by a German, Friedrich List, who had lived in the United States and was impressed by the rapid growth of its economy behind high tariff walls. He returned to Germany a passionate advocate of infant-industries protection for his native country. List conceded that free trade was best from a cosmopolitan standpoint, but argued that a nation could not afford to heed allocative arguments until it had developed its national industries. Only then, he argued, could a country take its rightful gains from the international division of labor. List's basic point was much like one put forth in Chapter 2: Comparative advantage has a time dimension, and the pattern of trade will reflect the *sequence* of national development. But List went much too far, insisting that countries can prosper only if they export manufactures and import foodstuffs. (Denmark, Australia, and New Zealand give the lie to this assertion; they export farm products yet have higher living standards than many industrial countries.) Unfortunately, List's argument not only won the day, but survives to bedevil economic policies in the less-developed countries of our own era. Many of these countries hanker after massive industries, although they could make better use of their scarce skills and capital. They confuse steel mills and oil refineries with prosperity and national identity.

France followed Germany in 1892, when a coalition of industry and agriculture reversed the low-tariff policies of Napoleon III and enacted the famous Méline Tariff to promote industrial development. The French economy grew rapidly after 1890, but the Méline Tariff cannot take credit for the upsurge. Indeed, it may have handicapped the iron and steel industry, as it levied a high tax on coal, raising the costs of the French iron manufacturers.[1]

[1]This point has to be learned anew by every generation, but may perhaps be easier to teach now that the economists have given it a fancy name. The "theory of effective protection" points out that tariffs on an industry's inputs reduce the net stimulus afforded that industry by the tariffs that are levied on its final outputs.

The resurgence of protectionism in the 1890's was followed by a period of tariff warfare involving Germany, Russia, Italy, and other countries. In 1902, Germany actually raised its tariff rates to obtain more leeway for bargaining, and peppered its tariff schedule with trivial distinctions to differentiate the exports of one country from those of another. To distinguish Swiss from Danish cattle, for example, the 1902 tariff had a separate category applying to "brown or dappled cows reared at a level of at least 300 metres above sea level and passing at least one month in every summer at an altitude of at least 800 metres." Hence, a reduction in the German tariff on Danish cattle would not automatically accrue to Swiss cattle under the *most-favored-nation* clause.

American tariffs did not come down as fast or far as European tariffs in the middle third of the nineteenth century. After 1860, moreover, they rose somewhat further. In 1861, Congress passed the Morrill Tariff Act, giving new protection to the iron and steel industry; in 1862 and 1864, it approved a sweeping increase in most other duties. When enacted, these new rates were not designed to grant more protection to American industry but merely to deny the foreigner an unfair advantage over U.S. producers; Congress had imposed heavy excise taxes on many domestic products to finance the Civil War, and the new import taxes were meant to offset them. When the war ended, however, and government spending declined, the domestic excise taxes were allowed to lapse, but the high import duties were not dismantled. They then came to exercise an awesome protective effect. American tariffs reached a postwar peak with the McKinley Tariff of 1890. They were brought down again during Cleveland's second term, when control of Congress passed briefly to the Democrats, but a Republican Congress pushed them to a new peak in 1897.

After 1900, the Republican party seemed to edge away from the extreme protectionism that had been one of its chief tenets. Its 1908 platform declared that "the true principle of protection is best maintined by the imposition of such duties as would equalize the difference between the cost of production at home and abroad, together with a reasonable degree of profit." This formula looked thoroughly reasonable and was reflected in the Tariff Act of 1909, which cut some duties slightly. But what you have already learned about foreign trade should show you that this "scientific" formula will often provide extravagant protection. Differences in costs are the basis for trade, and a tariff designed to offset those differences will therefore prohibit trade, save in tropical products and raw materials that are not produced domestically. If differences in national costs of production are offset by tariffs, transport costs will usually suffice to bar the import of foreign manufactures.

Collapse and Reconstruction: 1914–1939

On the eve of the First World War, the United States made a major tariff change. The Wilson administration reduced tariffs drastically in 1913 and added several items to the "free list," including iron, coal, raw wool, lumber, and news-

37

print. But the end of the World War brought massive new pressures for tariff protection here and abroad.

The war, and subsequent peace settlements, wrecked the international financial system. They disrupted established trade patterns and rearranged capital flows. They burdened the financial system with several layers of debt and large debt-service payments. The Allies had borrowed heavily in the United States to finance their purchases of war materiel. Then, the peace treaties levied reparations debts on the defeated nations. Europe's tariff frontiers were lengthened by some 12,000 miles as the old Habsburg Empire was chopped up into a half-dozen states —Czechoslovakia, Hungary, and the rest—each obliged to make its separate way in the world's market. And some of the victors suffered as much as the vanquished. Britain sold off many of its foreign assets to finance its war efforts, and was thereby deprived of the investment income that had served to offset the prewar decline in its major export industries.

To make matters worse, many American industries had expanded rapidly during the war, and they feared intense competition upon the end of hostilities. This was the case with the chemicals industry, the first to win extra protection after the war. The same thing happened in agriculture, here and in other countries. Encouraged to expand production during the war, farmers confronted ruinous competition afterward and faced adverse terms of trade throughout the 1920's. Rampant inflation compounded the general disorder. In 1923, a German housewife had to carry her money to market in a shopping bag, and could carry her groceries home in a change purse.

One by one, governments levied new tariffs. Some imposed outright import quotas. The new nations of Central Europe were among the first, but were not alone. Germany imposed a new agricultural tariff in 1925. The countries of Latin America applied tariffs and quotas much more freely than they had before the war. And Britain finally lapsed from free trade in 1919 and succumbed to systematic protection in 1931, amidst the general economic crisis.

The United States should have lowered its tariffs after the war, so that the outside world might earn more dollars to service its debts. Instead, Congress voted higher duties during the very first postwar slump. The Fordney–McCumber Tariff of 1922 was designed to aid the farmers, but also helped the chemicals industry and other "war babies."

The trend toward agricultural protection and quantitative trade controls continued in the second half of the decade. It was capped by our own Hawley–Smoot Tariff of 1930, once called the "Holy Smoke Tariff" by an undergraduate with more perception than memory. Congress began hearings on tariff reform in 1929, again intent on helping the farmers. But then the stock market collapsed and the economy began its sickening slide toward the Great Depression. One industry after another clamored for protection to stimulate employment, and when the new tariff bill was laid before Congress, an orgy of logrolling began. Congressmen traded votes with one another, seeking higher tariffs for their own constituents. When it was all over, the United States had the highest tariff in its history, and other countries were compelled to impose additional restrictions on imports from the United States. The Hawley–Smoot Tariff dashed all hopes for global recovery through expanded trade—hopes that had been fostered by the League of Nations' efforts to achieve a tariff truce.

The early 1930's gave birth to a new generation of trade controls. Struggling to prevent the spread of the depression, country after country cracked down on imports, seeking to stimulate domestic production by protecting business against foreign competition. Each in turn frustrated its neighbor's efforts; a fall in one country's imports meant a fall in another country's exports. And after Great Britain had devalued the pound in 1931 and the United States had devalued the dollar in 1934, France and other European countries began to use import controls to defend their currencies.

Foreign trade lagged far behind industrial production in the slow recovery from the Great Depression. It was, indeed, a drag rather than a stimulant to faster expansion. In 1928, world imports had totaled $60 billion; in 1938, they were a mere $25 billion—less than half the predepression level.

After 1932, U.S. import duties started to decline. A part of this reduction was caused by an increase in prices during the recovery. Many U.S. tariffs are *specific* duties, fixed in cents per pound, dollars per dozen, and so on. When prices fall, their *ad valorem* (percentage) equivalents rise; when prices rise, those equivalents fall. A 50¢ tariff on a $10 product works out to 5 per cent; if the price falls to $5, the duty works out to 10 per cent; if the price rises to $20, the duty works out to 2.5 per cent.

But the decline in American tariffs was also caused by a major turnabout in policy. Casting about for ways to increase employment, the Roosevelt administration finally turned to world markets, launching a campaign to reduce trade barriers and expand U.S. exports. In 1934, President Roosevelt asked Congress for the power to negotiate bilateral trade agreements that would cut American tariffs by as much as half in return for equivalent reductions by other countries. The President told Congress:

> A resumption of international trade cannot but improve the general situation of other countries, and thus increase their purchasing power. Let us well remember that this in turn spells increased opportunity for American sales. . . . Legislation such as this is an essential step in the program of national economic recovery which the Congress has elaborated during this past year.

Roosevelt promised that tariff reductions would not injure American producers—that he would not open American markets to competitive imports. In effect, he forswore the allocative gains from trade, looking instead for effects on employment through an expansion of exports. He apparently planned to bargain away our *surplus* protection—the rates that could be cut without attracting imports. Congress gave him the powers he wanted, and the United States nego-

39

tiated 31 trade agreements with other governments. In each case, moreover, it extended its own concessions to other trading countries under the *most-favored-nation* clause. The Trade Agreements Program was much like the network of treaties that spread out from France following the Cobden–Chevalier Treaty of 1860. Unlike that earlier system, however, it did not bring the nations close to free trade: in 1939, the average U.S. tariff was just below what it had been a decade before, on the eve of the Hawley–Smoot debacle.

The Trade Agreements Program did, however, help to arrest the world-wide increase in tariffs that had been choking world trade. It also held our own tariffs down during and after the Second World War. (After every other major war, by contrast, the U.S. tariff had risen substantially.) This accomplishment was all the more impressive because the inflation of the 1940's greatly reduced the *ad valorem* value of specific duties. By 1945, the average American tariff was as low as it had been in 1919 (see Fig. 3–1).

THE MULTILATERAL APPROACH TO TRADE POLICY

The American Initiative

The Second World War damaged world trade even more than had the Great Depression. Most of the belligerents imposed strict *exchange controls* to prevent their citizens from spending foreign currencies needed to purchase war materiel and food. They then carried their controls into the postwar period in order to save scarce foreign currencies for their reconstruction programs.

Very early in the war, however, experts began to draw plans for the liberalization of foreign trade and payments in the postwar period. Even before the fighting stopped, the Allied governments established two new financial institutions, the International Monetary Fund (IMF) and the International Bank for Reconstruction and development (IBRD), to revive and sustain the payments system and to encourage flows of long-term capital. They also planned to promote a fast recovery of world trade by joint action to relax the complex controls that had slowed recovery in the 1930's and strangled trade during the war.

The experts found serious flaws in the prewar Trade Agreements Program. Many governments had withheld tariff concessions from the United States to save some bargaining power for subsequent negotiations with other countries. The war-time planners consequently urged the use of *multilateral* agreements rather than a new set of country-by-country pacts. Each government might then weigh all it had won—the concessions it had obtained directly in return for its own, and those it had obtained indirectly under the *most-favored-nation* clause. The experts also sought ways to remove the import quotas, payments agreements, and other trade controls that had been used abroad in lieu of tariffs. Quotas frustrate the price system by barring imports, no matter how cheap. Tariffs, by contrast,

40

handicap the foreigner but do not freeze trade patterns or prevent price changes from affecting the allocation of resources. Furthermore, quotas were sometimes used to nullify negotiated tariff cuts: governments imposed import quotas after they had cut their duties. The United States consequently sought a comprehensive agreement on commercial policy, and not just new tariff treaties.

The new U.S. trade policy found its first expression in wartime agreements between the United States and Great Britain—in the Atlantic Charter and Lend-Lease Agreement. It was then embodied in a charter for an International Trade Organization (ITO) to be affiliated with the United Nations. But the ITO never came into being. Its charter was too long and complicated, and was perforated by a host of exceptions and qualifications. It antagonized the foes of international cooperation, who charged that the ITO would meddle with domestic economic policies. It antagonized the advocates of cooperation, who complained that the exceptions and qualifications had swamped the principles, and that no one would be bound to obey the rules.

In 1947, however, the major trading countries were able to agree on interim rules, and began a series of conferences to reduce tariffs and to dismantle other barriers. This interim arrangement has survived, and is known as the General Agreement on Tariffs and Trade (GATT). The GATT is a comparatively simple document; it does not seek to deal with every issue or to anticipate every contingency. Its heart is the *most-favored-nation* clause, which provides that every tariff bargain made at GATT meetings shall be extended to all member countries.

This clause increases each country's willingness to make concessions. Each government that grants a tariff concession to another knows that it will receive the benefit of any concession granted by the other to a third and, indeed, the benefit of all bargains struck. GATT also militates against withdrawal of concessions already granted, as all the countries injured by the withdrawal are entitled, under GATT rules, to withdraw concessions from the offending nation. (The notion that lowering a tariff is a concession, causing internal injury that calls for a reciprocal concession, illustrates the pervasive, tenacious survival of protectionist semantics. In our consideration of tariff bargaining, we should not forget the benefits of free trade.)

The GATT commercial code outlaws discriminatory tariffs and prohibits the use of import quotas except by countries experiencing balance-of-payments problems, or by those imposing similar quotas on domestic production—on farm products, for example. It allows the less-developed countries to protect their infant industries, but subjects them to regular GATT review. Finally, it provides machinery to resolve disputes arising from trade policy and to press for the liberalization of trade practices. GATT has battered away at the "hard-core" quotas that some West European nations retained long after the original balance-of-payments justification for them had disappeared. GATT has also worked on disentangling problems raised by the creation of the European Economic Community, or Common Market. The formation of the Common Market has threat-

41

ened the interests of outsiders, including the United States, and GATT members have asked the European countries to adjust their policies so as to minimize damage and dislocation.

Obstacles to Tariff Bargaining

In 1945, Congress passed another Trade Agreements Act, authorizing the President to reduce American tariffs through new international bargaining. The United States participated in five GATT conferences between 1947 and 1961. The largest tariff cuts came at the first two, held in 1947 and in 1948, when the United States could negotiate under the liberal bargaining authority of the 1945 Act, permitting cuts as large as 50 per cent. The Europeans were quite willing to make large concessions at those same two meetings, as Europe's trade was still controlled by absolute quotas and currency restrictions. To see how these GATT meetings affected U.S. tariffs, compare the last two columns in Table 3–1; duties declined in every major category, and some rates fell substantially.

Table 3–1 TARIFF REDUCTIONS SINCE 1934, BY COMMODITY CLASS
(duties collected as a percentage of 1952 dutiable imports)

Commodity Class	1934	1945	1953
All dutiable imports	24.4	17.9	12.2
Chemicals, oils, and paints	25.1	20.0	12.4
Earthenware and glassware	40.6	36.7	24.7
Metals and metal products	23.7	18.9	12.1
Wood and wood products	10.9	7.5	4.7
Sugar and molasses	25.8	13.5	9.4
Tobacco and tobacco products	45.6	34.7	20.3
Agricultural products	16.2	12.5	9.4
Spirits, wines, and other beverages	81.4	41.6	23.1
Cotton products	36.8	30.0	21.8
Flax, hemp, and jute	12.2	9.0	5.2
Wool and wool products	36.7	30.2	22.4
Silk products	58.8	52.7	31.0
Synthetic-fiber textiles	32.8	31.0	17.7
Pulp, paper, and books	20.4	15.2	9.4
Sundries	31.8	26.5	19.1

Source: United States Tariff Commission, "Effect of Trade Agreement Concessions on United States Tariff Levels," 1954.

American imports did not respond to these postwar tariff cuts until other countries had repaired war damage and could increase exports. Recently, however, dutiable imports have been growing faster than duty-free imports, and there has been a considerable rise in manufactured imports, due partly to the tariff reductions negotiated at GATT meetings.

U.S. tariffs changed very little between the GATT negotiations of 1950–1951 and those of 1960–1961 with the Common Market. This was because the

American negotiators could not offer large reductions in the 1950's, as Congress had amended the Trade Agreements Act to limit their authority.

When President Roosevelt first asked for the authority to reduce U.S. tariffs, he promised that no injury would befall American industry. When President Truman requested additional tariff-cutting powers in 1945, he renewed this pledge. But Truman's assurances did not satisfy Congress, and when the Trade Agreements Act had to be renewed again in 1947, the President was compelled to introduce formal procedures for dealing with injury. He asked the Tariff Commission, a six-man board appointed by the President, to weigh any evidence of injury brought forward by individual industries, and, when it had sufficient evidence, to recommend an increase in tariffs or other import restrictions. The President reserved the right to set aside its findings, but had put himself on the defensive. He would henceforth have to justify refusing additional protection.

Protectionist sentiment grew stronger in the early 1950's. With the reconstruction of war-damaged industries abroad, American producers began to meet vigorous competition from Europe and Japan. In addition, labor unions were beginning to worry about low foreign wages. And some Southern congressmen had abandoned their historic opposition to high tariffs; as the South experienced industrial development, they rediscovered the infant-industries argument. In 1951, Congress wrote an *escape clause* into the Trade Agreements Act, formalizing the procedures established by the President and listing the criteria to be used in appraising a complaint of injury:

> In arriving at a determination . . . the Tariff Commission, without excluding other factors, shall take into consideration a downward trend of production, employment, prices, profits, or wages in the domestic industry concerned, or a decline in sales, an increase in imports, either actual or relative to domestic production, a higher or growing inventory, or a decline in the proportion of the domestic market supplied by domestic producers.

Notice that an increase in imports was to be regarded as a *measure* of injury, not just a cause, and that it did not have to be an absolute increase or at the expense of domestic production. A company could petition for higher tariffs if its sales had increased but imports had increased faster.

In 1955 and 1958, Congress broadened the escape clause and made it more difficult for the President to reject the advice of the Tariff Commission. It also wrote a National Security Amendment into the law:

> . . . The President shall . . . give consideration to domestic production needed for projected national defense requirements, . . . existing and anticipated availabilities of the human resources, products, raw materials, and other supplies and services essential to the national defense, and the requirements of growth in such . . . supplies and services including the investment, exploration, and development necessary to assure such growth, . . . and shall take into consideration the impact of foreign competition on the economic welfare of individual domestic industries . . . in determining whether such weakening of our internal economy may impair the national security.

43

This amendment made very little sense. Economists have always endorsed the protection of defense-related industries. Adam Smith himself supported Britain's *Navigation Acts* because "the defense of Great Britain . . . depends very much upon the number of its sailors and shipping." In our day, however, a nation's security depends on the arsenal of weapons it has built up before hostilities start. This country's power to combat aggression is not enhanced by protecting the domestic producers of watches, lead and zinc, or oil, and sustaining their skills for use in arms production the day after someone has dropped The Bomb. But the sweeping phrases of the National Security Amendment were really designed to serve a more general purpose—to erect one more barrier against import competition. Incidentally, it has been invoked only once—to put quotas on imports of petroleum, including residual fuel oil used in household and industrial furnaces. These quotas were ostensibly designed to stimulate the search for additional domestic petroleum deposits, but also protected the soft-coal industry which has been badly injured by the changeover from coal to fuel oil.

The escape clause and National Security Amendment gave relief from injury after it had happened—so another clause was added to the Trade Agreements Act to forestall injury. This clause, the *peril-point* provision, directed the President to list all the products on which he planned to make concessions at GATT meetings, so that the Tariff Commission might decide what duties might be needed to prevent injury. The President could then cut a tariff far below its "peril point"—though he would be obliged to give his reasons in a special message to Congress.

These postwar amendments to U.S. trade policy prevented large-scale tariff reductions for a full decade. Furthermore, several of our duties were raised, damaging U.S. relations with friendly countries. Switzerland was injured and offended by an increase in the tariff on watches. Belgium expressed serious doubts about our sincerity in tariff bargaining when, just after making a major agreement with the European Common Market, the United States applied new tariffs to Belgian carpets. The escape clause and National Security Amendment also served to warn our trading partners that past tariff concessions might be snatched away if they were exploited too successfully, while the peril-point provision sometimes caused other countries to withhold concessions because the United States could not reply in kind. In 1960–1961, for example, the Common Market proposed a 20 per cent reduction in its common external tariff if the United States would make a similar reduction. When it became clear that the American negotiators could not make so broad a cut, the Europeans pared down their offer.

The European Initiative

44   Each time the White House asked for a renewal of the Trade Agreements Act, a parade of industry spokesmen appeared before congressional committees

to demand more protection and to denounce low tariffs as the source of all their woes. Each time, the administration purchased a renewal of its bargaining powers by agreeing to amendments that restricted its freedom of action and provided easier ways to redress injury.

Yet the advocates of liberal tariff policies were not wholly dissatisfied with this ritual. They argued that tariffs were not too important—that quotas and limitations on the convertibility of foreign currencies were doing much more damage to world trade. They also pointed out that few foreign countries could offer much in tariff bargaining, for their markets were too small. These were valid views of the situation in the early 1950's. But as the United States marked time in trade policy, events in Europe were undermining the premises of U.S. policy. European governments were making dramatic decisions that would change the balance of advantage in tariff bargaining. By the 1960's, most experts agreed, American industry had far more to gain than lose from new negotiations.

At the close of the Second World War, the United States began an unprecedented financial effort to reconstruct Western Europe. This was the Marshall Plan. At the same time, it urged the Europeans to combine their resources and realize an age-old dream: a United States of Europe. Washington was much concerned to strengthen Europe against Soviet aggression, and, as urgently, to enlist Germany in a democratic federation so that it might never destroy the peace again.

At first, the Europeans started to integrate one industry at a time—the sector-by-sector approach to unification. They established a European Coal and Steel Community, making for free trade in coal and steel and creating a supranational High Authority with the power to regulate pricing policies and commercial practices. Then they changed their tactics and began to work for a full *customs union* of six continental countries—France, Germany, Italy, the Netherlands, Belgium, and Luxembourg. In 1957 these countries signed the Treaty of Rome, establishing the European Economic Community (EEC), or Common Market. They agreed to eliminate all barriers to trade among themselves and to surround themseves with a common external tariff—a set of duties constructed by averaging their separate national tariffs.

The EEC planned to achieve internal free trade by 1970, by a series of staged tariff reductions. Because of swift progress in the early years, and despite later crises, the custom unions and the common external tariff went into effect July 1, 1968. The EEC also agreed to harmonize domestic policies, including agricultural policies, to lift their restrictions on movements of men and money inside Europe, and to plan for political unification. In 1958, the Europeans took another major step. They made their currencies fully convertible, removing any cause for continued discrimination against American goods. Once their currencies could be used freely to buy dollars, no country had reason to require that its citizens buy European goods to conserve dollar earnings. In consequence, most countries lifted their import quotas.

45

For many Europeans, and for Washington as well, eventual political unification is the chief rationale for the EEC. But the member countries also hope to reap large economic gains. They expect to sharpen business competiton, thereby to foster a more efficient use of resources and a better allocation of economic tasks. They expect to capture the economies of scale often associated with larger markets and, in consequence, to strengthen European firms *vis-à-vis* the "giant-sized" American companies. The European Common Market has a combined population of about 185,000,000 and a gross regional product approaching $350 billion; it is nearly as populous as the United States, and is almost half as wealthy.

The transition to internal free trade and policy harmonization has been neither smooth nor painless. It has in fact been punctuated by several crises, the first of which occurred in 1963 when France exercised its veto power to reject Britain's first application for membership. Divisions over agricultural policy have precipitated several crises; one (in 1965–66) nearly split the EEC, as the French boycotted important Community functions. The Treaty of Rome called for a Common Agricultural Policy (CAP) that would ensure a "fair" standard of living for farmers. The domestic political power of the farmers in each member country drastically reduced the possibility of mutual concessions, driving the governments into sharp confrontations. The CAP that finally came into effect in July 1968 establishes a single price throughout the EEC for all agricultural products, with prices supported, where necessary, by government programs. A central EEC fund pays for the governments' programs and also subsidizes exports of surplus commodities. Finally, agricultural imports are regulated by a *variable levy* equal to the difference between the world price and the EEC support price. One major negotiating issue was the height of the common support price for grains. The Germans want high community prices to protect their relatively inefficient farmers; the French want low ones to enlarge French exports of grains to Germany. The EEC compromised on a price midway between the two countries' national levels. The French have drawn the largest amount of Community funds for their domestic support programs, and the Germans have contributed the most.

Despite agreement on the CAP, trouble seems inevitable. The EEC is accumulating huge stocks of dairy products (mostly French), and spending large sums of money to maintain dairy and other prices. Some Europeans are beginning to realize that a rational agricultural policy would try to move farmers into more productive, industrial occupations. A more immediate issue of contention, the financing of the CAP, is soon to be reopened and promises new confrontations as the Germans and Italians wish to limit the rising costs of price supports, of which they pay the largest share.

Lurking behind these particular issues is a more serious, general obstacle to policy harmonization: the French government of General de Gaulle was deeply suspicious of all supranational arrangements, for they involve the sacrifice of national autonomy. It had sought to curb the powers of the EEC Commission, the civil service of the Community. Now that de Gaulle has passed from the political scene there may be new efforts to speed integration, and the question of British entry has now been reopened. The General's veto in 1963 was repeated in 1967 and in 1968. He feared that British entry would alter substantially the balance of power within the EEC and might greatly affect EEC policy towards outsiders. British entry would also lead to the entry of some of Britain's partners in the European Free Trade Association (EFTA),[2] greatly enlarging the EEC and changing its character.

The United States and the EEC

The formation of the EEC, the world's largest trading bloc, vastly affects trade and investment patterns in the rest of the world. Western Europe's rapid economic growth has been a magnet for private American capital. The recorded value of American corporate investments in the EEC, less than $2 billion in 1958, jumped to nearly $9 billion by 1968. Many American industries now manufacture more abroad, mainly in Europe, than they export from plants in the United States, and overseas production continues to grow rapidly. American capital has been attracted by both the high rate of growth and the opportunity to produce and sell inside the EEC tariff wall.

The effects of the EEC on U.S. exports are a source of some concern. The EEC common tariff may not be higher than the separate national tariffs from which it was built, but it can nevertheless divert trade from American exports. Previously, exports from the United States to France paid the same tariff as exports from Germany or Italy, but now France's EEC partners pay no tariffs at all, whereas goods from the United States and other outsiders are still taxed. An additional complication is the "associate" status the EEC has granted to some of the less-developed countries, mostly former colonies in Africa, admitting their exports on preferential terms that damage trade from other developing countries, mostly in Latin America.

The American government, worried about *its* farmers, has strenuously objected to EEC agricultural policy. The variable levy is a damaging novelty among protectionist devices, for any lowering of world prices is offset by an increase in the levy. The standard EEC response to all objections is that the higher growth stimulated by formation of the Community will encourage imports from outside and offset the trade diversion that outsiders fear. Since the formation of the EEC, American exports to the Community have indeed grown substantially, and have also increased as a percentage of total U.S. exports— they rose from 13.6 per cent in 1958 to 18.0 per cent in 1967. Nevertheless, the American share in total EEC *imports* was lower in 1967 than 1958–59, falling from 12.2 per cent to 10.7 per cent. One very careful investigation has concluded that total loss of manufactured exports due to the formation of the EEC has been very small, taking account of both trade diversion and the faster

[2]The other members of EFTA are Sweden, Denmark, Norway, Austria, Portugal, and Switzerland. Within EFTA, there is free trade, but each country maintains its own external tariff.

growth of the EEC, but that losses of agricultural exports may exceed $2 billion in the period 1958–70.

Responding to European developments, the Kennedy administration decided to seek new tariff legislation, and in the Trade Expansion Act of 1962, Congress authorized the president to cut U.S. tariffs once again. In fact, it gave him much more power than it had conferred by any single tariff law since the original Trade Agreements Act of 1934. Heretofore the United States had bargained on a rate-by-rate, product-by-product basis; henceforth, it could make more sweeping agreements: it could cut *all* its tariffs in half, in return for similar "across-the-board" reductions by other countries. Furthermore, the Trade Expansion Act modified the basic "no injury" rule that had hobbled U.S. negotiators and impaired the logic of our tariff policy. A country exports so that it can import, yet the old Trade Agreements Acts were chiefly concerned to stimulate exports. They looked on additional imports as the price we had to pay to widen our export markets—and one we would not pay if increased imports damaged domestic industry. The 1962 law makes much more sense. First, it redefines injury from imports, instructing the Tariff Commission to require evidence that men and machines have actually been idled by foreign competition—not merely that prices have fallen or that imports have grown faster than domestic production. Second, it provides new ways to deal with injury. Instead of imposing additional tariffs, the President may authorize direct assistance: extended unemployment compensation and retraining for workers; tax benefits and loans for employers, to help them diversify or modernize their plants. Thus, it seeks to capture the allocative gains from trade by fostering changes in resource use, rather than renouncing those important gains by restricting foreign trade and subsidizing inefficient industries.

Soon after the passage of the Trade Expansion Act, a new round of bargaining got underway. It was interrupted several times by the internal crises of the EEC; its ultimate success, in May 1967, not long before American bargaining authority would have expired, was in doubt until the very end. All sides wanted to avert a breakdown in the talks, as collapse of the so-called "Kennedy round" would have been a major setback for the world economy, whereas freer trade would improve the allocation of resources within the industrial world, and would provide the less-developed countries with a new stimulus to economic growth.

Success in the protracted negotiations depended in the main on the EEC and the United States, and they were at first divided on a host of complex issues. The two thorniest were "disparities" in tariff levels on manufactured goods and the EEC's agricultural policy. The Europeans claimed that uniform 50 per cent cuts in tariffs on all manufactures would penalize them. They argued that although the *average* tariff levels of the United States and the EEC were roughly the same, the EEC's common external tariff was concentrated in a range (between 10 and 20 per cent) where a uniform 50 per cent cut would have a substantial effect on imports, whereas U.S. tariffs were widely dispersed around the average, minimizing the impact of a uniform reduction. A 50 per cent reduction in a 40 per cent tariff, they argued, would not increase imports much, whereas the total elimination of a 5 per cent tariff would be of little significance. The EEC reasoning is hard to accept, for the impact of a tariff reduction depends on the relative size of the cut, not on the initial height of the tariff. The EEC, however, held to its position, and the negotiators agreed to allow all parties to deposit a significant list of "exceptions" to the uniform 50 per cent cut.

Agriculture caused the other major erosion in uniformity. After assembling its farm policy with so much difficulty, the EEC was not disposed to unravel it by accepting across-the-board reductions in agricultural duties. In the end, the major parties agreed to a "pragmatic" solution, involving item-by-item negotiations, and these nearly collapsed when they came to trade in grains. The United States insisted on guaranteed access to a constant share of the EEC grains market, equal to its then-current share. The EEC offered much less. For the sake of salvaging the Kennedy Round, the grains issue was left unresolved.

Looking at manufactures, the Kennedy Round was a substantial success. Two thirds of the duty reductions (measured by the value of the trade involved) were 50 per cent or more and embraced the principal industrial countries. The overall average tariff reduction on manufactures (taking account of the "exceptions") was about 33 per cent. The EEC granted concessions on more than 90 per cent of all its manufactured imports from the United States, the average reduction amounting again to 33 per cent. Looking at agriculture, there was less cause for jubilation. The United States obtained concessions on products accounting for 25 per cent of the EEC's agricultural imports from the United States, but the EEC declined to modify its restrictive and expensive price support policy or to abandon the variable levy.

Current Trade Problems

Many issues in trade policy remain outstanding, despite the great success of the Kennedy Round. The United States and the other industrialized nations have barely begun an assault on nontariff barriers to trade. These barriers take many forms, including customs formalities, labeling requirements, outmoded sanitary regulations, and government procurement policies. Our own Buy American Act, for example, instructs the American government to buy from domestic sources even when much cheaper foreign goods are available. The United States is particularly anxious to remove quotas on its goods, which many major countries still impose in violation of GATT rules. Japan maintains quotas on more than 130 American products, including computers, color film, and leather goods. The United States also wants further talks on agriculture, hoping to make a dent in the EEC's protectionist policies.

At the same time, unfortunately, the United States seems to be in the grip

49

of a protectionist renascence. The ink was barely dry on the Kennedy Round agreement before a series of bills, imposing import quotas on a long list of products, was introduced by individual members of Congress. At one point, quota bills for steel, textiles, petroleum, watches, lead, zinc, meat, and dairy products were pending in Congress, affecting some $6 billion of imports and threatening to unleash the wildest protectionist logrolling since the days of Hawley–Smoot. Our trading partners protested loudly, pointing out that Congress could not in good faith enact legislation negating tariff concessions negotiated under Congressional authority. They drove the moral lesson home by providing lists of American exports that would suffer retaliation, permitted by GATT, if the bills passed. These objections stalled the protectionists' drive, but the pressures that still exist have led two administrations to mollify the protectionists by negotiating "voluntary" agreements with other countries to limit certain exports to the United States. Most major steel exporters (Japan and the European Coal and Steel Community) have accepted a "voluntary" limit on steel exports. The United States has been trying to persuade major textile exporters to accept "voluntary" quotas (on cotton goods, already limited, plus wool and synthetics). Textile restrictions of this kind, even when they limit only the growth of imports, would hurt the development efforts of countries that have successfully managed to sell in the American market. The resistance to "voluntary" quotas has led the President to ask Congress for authority to impose quotas on textile imports. Moreover, Congress is anxious to grant, against the President's wishes, quotas on a wide range of goods.

Congressional concern is based, of course, on fears that a flood of imports will hurt American business and destroy jobs. The proper response to imports, however, is not to restrict them but to reallocate resources displaced from import-competing industries, using the adjustment assistance provisions of the Trade Expansion Act. We have also to make sure that the American economy is growing steadily. Companies will not diversify production if they lack new markets; workers will not benefit from retraining if there are no new jobs. European experience has itself demonstrated that an adjustment to import competition is easiest when aggregate demand is growing rapidly, so that opportunities abound for those who lose their jobs. If indeed there is any reason to insist that the American economy grow fast, it is that rapid growth will permit adjustments to all sorts of disturbances: changes in tastes and technology, and increased import competition. The pull of buoyant demand is much more effective in reshuffling resources than is the sting of shrinking markets and high unemployment.

SUMMARY

The tariff histories of Western Europe and the United States describe very similar cycles. Both histories reflect the influence of economic theory, industrial development, and international politics.

In Europe, tariffs started downward after the Napoleonic Wars, reaching their nadir after 1860. Britain led the way with unilateral reductions; the continental countries followed suit, using tariff treaties. Tariffs moved up again after 1880, with the re-emergence of aggressive nationalism and shifts in the balance of political power caused partly by shifts in agricultural trade. Trade restrictions became even more severe in the 1920's, and the global depression of the 1930's caused many countries to impose import quotas. These controls remained in force through the Second World War, but were gradually dismantled in the 1950's. Then, Europe began to cut its tariff rates as well, chiefly in respect to European trade, not on imports from outside. The European Economic Community, or Common Market, is the end-product of this trend. It has eliminated all trade barriers within Western Europe and will facilitate the free flow of labor and capital.

In the United States, tariffs moved upward after the Napoleonic Wars, and came down briefly during the 1840's and 1850's, coincident with the repeal of the British Corn Laws. But they moved up again during the Civil War, and did not decline until the eve of the First World War. Afterward, moreover, U.S. tariffs rose again, hitting their all-time high with the Hawley–Smoot Tariff of 1930. Thereafter, the United States negotiated tariff treaties with a large number of countries, and in the 1940's and 1950's participated in new tariff bargaining under the auspices of the General Agreement on Tariffs and Trade. The U.S. program lost momentum in the 1950's as Congress added restrictive amendments to the Trade Agreements Act: the escape clause, the peril-point provision, and the National Security Amendment. In 1962, however, Congress passed new trade legislation, responding to the challenge of the EEC. The legislation produced the successful Kennedy Round of tariff negotiations which culminated in major worldwide tariff reductions.

The Balance of Payments

and Foreign-Exchange Market

CHAPTER FOUR

BALANCE-OF-PAYMENTS
ACCOUNTING

Thus far, we have studied the effects of foreign trade on the allocation of resources and distribution of income—always assuming that payments from one country to another are balanced by payments from the second to the first. This vital equality can be secured by wage-rate or exchange-rate changes. In Chapter 2, you will recall, American wage rates and prices were at first so low that consumers in both America and Britain preferred to buy American coal but were indifferent as between American or British potatoes. Trade did not balance. Then the foreign demand for American coal raised America's wage rate until its potatoes became more expensive than British potatoes, and balanced trade ensued. As a matter of actual fact, however, wage rates and prices may not respond smoothly to correct imbalances in international payments. Wages and other costs may be very sticky and may even move independently of demand conditions, *causing* a lopsided flow of payments. Furthermore, some international cash flows will not act on wages and prices so as to restore equilibrium; a demand for foreign securities, for example, will not change wage rates or other costs directly.

Under these circumstances, governments seeking to maintain fixed exchange rates may encounter difficult monetary problems in their relations with the outside world. Economists sometimes describe these problems as "transitional" or "short-run" phenomena that should not divert our attention from the "real" flows of goods, services, and capital. But the "short run" may drag on for a long time, and imperfections in the process of wage, price, and exchange-rate adjustment may often alter "real" flows. If wage rates and exchange rates are rigid, a country may not be able to balance its external transactions at a satisfactory level of domestic employment or may have to forego economic growth. In the late 1950's for example, the condition of the U.S. *balance of payments,* or sum total of American transactions with foreigners, discouraged the government from adopting financial policies to stimulate domestic growth.

As a preface to our study of these monetary issues, we will examine a group of transactions put together in a hypothetical *balance-of-payments* table for the United States. Then we will consider the several ways of balancing the cash flows that arise from these transactions.

A balance-of-payments table is designed to summarize a nation's transactions with the outside world. It is usually divided into three sections:

1. *The current account,* which shows flows of goods and services.
2. *The capital account,* which shows lending and investment.
3. *The cash account,* which shows how cash balances and short-term claims have changed in response to current and capital transactions.

All balance-of-payments transactions are classified as either *credits* (entered with a plus sign) or *debits* (entered with a minus sign). An American export is treated as credit because it generates a foreign payment for American goods or services. An American import is a debit because it creates an American payment for foreign goods. Transactions classified under current account include not only exports and imports of physical merchandise but also "invisible" items, such as tourist expenditures (an American paying for his hotel room in London is buying British services), shipping and insurance services, and interest and dividends earned on foreign investments. An item is a credit when it necessitates a payment to the United States and a debit when it necessitates a payment to foreigners. A credit item will generate a foreign demand for dollars; a debit an American demand for foreign currency.

All current-account transactions affect real income. Foreign spending on current American output is equal to our exports of domestic goods and services, and it measures the foreign impact on domestic output and employment. Similarly, American imports of goods and services constitute a demand for foreign output. Other current-account items, such as income on foreign assets, also create income but do not constitute an immediate demand for a country's goods and services.

Transactions on capital account affect wealth and debt. An American acquiring foreign stocks and bonds is acquiring claims on foreigners, and will earn future income from his ownership of these claims. His purchases of these securities are classified on capital account. Government lending, as under foreign aid programs, is also classified on capital account, since the U.S. government acquires a claim on future foreign income. Note carefully that an American purchase of a foreign security or an interest in a foreign company (American

53

lending or investment) is classified in the balance of payments as a debit. An increase in American claims on foreigners necessitates a payment to acquire foreign assets (just as an import necessitates a payment to acquire foreign goods) and is a debit. Foreign lending and investment in the United States is, for symmetrical reasons, classified as a credit. Looking at current and capital account together, an item is a credit if it is a purchase of U.S. goods, services, or assets (claims on the United States); it is a debit if it is an American purchase of foreign goods, services, or assets (claims on foreigners).

All current and capital account transactions must have cash or credit counterparts. For example, a foreigner can pay for an American export by running down his (or his bank's) dollar holdings or by obtaining a short-term dollar credit. A decrease in foreign dollar holdings is, of course, a decrease in foreign claims on the United States and an American credit to a foreigner is an increase in American claims on foreigners. We have already learned to call these debits. An American import can be paid for by running down our foreign-currency holdings or by increasing our indebtedness to foreigners. Both transactions are credits. Thus, each credit transaction has, as its double-entry bookkeeping counterpart, a debit. A positive sum (a net credit) for all current and capital account transactions will be called a *balance-of-payments surplus*. The corresponding net increase in American claims on foreigners and decrease in foreign claims on Americans (a net debit) must appear in the cash account; it constitutes financing for the surplus.[1] A negative sum of current and capital account transactions indicates a *balance-of-payments deficit* and will be matched by a net decrease in American cash claims on foreigners and increase in foreign cash claims on Americans.

Table 4–1 is a hypothetical balance-of-payments table for the United States. It illustrates these accounting principles by way of five transactions:

1. *An American purchase of $240,000 worth of tin from Malaya, paid for with pounds sterling bought with dollars from a New York bank.*

The purchase of tin will appear on current account because it creates income abroad. It will appear as a *debit* there because it enlarges the supply of goods available to Americans. It is listed next to *merchandise imports* in Table 4–1. The transfer of pounds sterling to pay for the tin will appear on cash account

---

[1]Notice that some external claims are considered capital and some cash, or short-term claims, and put into the cash account. Classification problems arise frequently.

Some foreign debts and claims are easily classified. The purchase of a permanent interest in a foreign company is a long-term capital transaction. The acquisition of a foreign bank balance is a cash transaction. But how should a foreign purchase of a U.S. Treasury bill be classified? It is an earning asset for the foreigner, just like a bond or stock, but is a close substitute for cash because it matures very quickly. Many foreign banks and governments invest their dollar holdings in short-term securities like Treasury bills, rather than holding idle bank deposits. In practice, the dividing line between capital and cash is drawn so that claims and debts maturing in a year or less go into the cash account, and those that mature in more than a year (or have no fixed maturity) go into the capital account. Like any arbitrary rule, this one sometimes leads to strange results. But we need some sort of rule to assure consistency and permit comparisons through time.

Table 4–1   A HYPOTHETICAL BALANCE-OF-PAYMENTS TABLE FOR THE UNITED STATES (thousands of dollars)

Item		Amount
A. Current Account		
Merchandise exports		+500
Antibiotics	300	
Machine tools	200	
Merchandise imports		−240
Tin	240	
Services		+50
Ship rental	50	
Balance on current account		+310
B. Capital Account		
Direct investment		−400
Factory in Italy	400	
Government lending		−200
Indian loan	200	
Balance on capital account		−600
Balance on current and capital accounts		−290
C. Cash Account		
Increase (+) in foreign holdings of dollars		+100
Antibiotics	−300	
Factory in Italy	400	
Indian loan	200	
Machine tools	−200	
Increase (−) in U.S. holdings of foreign currencies		+190
Tin	240	
Ship rental	−50	
Balance on cash account		+290

as a change in *U.S. holdings of foreign currencies*. It will appear as a *credit* there because it reduces American claims on the outside world (U.S. holdings of pounds sterling). The American importer of tin will go to a New York bank, write a check for $240,000 (plus a small commission), and receive a *draft* for £100,000 drawn on that bank's balance at a London bank. The ratio $240: £100 or $2.40: £1 is the exchange rate between the dollar and the pound. Next, the American importer will transfer the sterling draft to the Malayan tin producer, who will sell it to his bank in Singapore, obtaining the Malayan equivalent of £100,000. To complete the transaction, the bank in Singapore will send the draft to London, where the bank on which it was drawn will deduct £100,000 from the sterling balance of the New York bank that issued the draft.

2. *An American sale of $300,000 worth of antibiotics to Venezuela, paid for with dollars bought from a bank in Caracas.*

The American sales of antibiotics will also appear on current account, because it creates income in the United States. But it will be a *credit* item because it decreases the supply of goods available to Americans. It is listed next

55

to *merchandise exports* in Table 4–1. The transfer of dollars to pay for the drugs will show up in the cash account as a change in *foreign holdings of dollars,* and will be a *debit* there because it decreases American liabilities to the outside world (Venezuelan holdings of dollars). In this case, the Venezuelan importer will buy a $300,000 draft from a bank in Caracas, paying with Venezuelan currency. He will send the dollar draft to the U.S. exporter, who will deposit it in his own bank. The draft will then be sent to the New York bank at which the Venezuelan bank keeps its dollar balance, and $300,000 will be deducted from the Venezuelan's dollar account.

3. *The leasing of an American ship for $50,000 to carry frozen beef from Argentina to Liverpool.*

This transaction is similar to an export sale; the U.S. shipowner contracts to provide a service using American resources. Hence, the rental fee will appear as a *credit* on current account. If, next, the Argentine meatpacker leasing the ship pays $50,000 worth of Argentine currency (pesos) and the U.S. shipowner sells them to his bank, there will be an increase in American holdings of Argentine currency, and this will appear as a *debit* (an increase of American claims on foreigners) in the cash account of Table 4–1.

4. *The building of a $400,000 factory in Italy by an American company, to assemble tractors for sale in the Common Market.*

This transaction also appears in the U.S. balance of payments, although no goods or services cross our own frontier. It represents the acquisition of an earning asset, and will appear as a *debit* on capital account. It is called *direct investment* because it is an outright extension of American enterprise rather than a purchase of securities issued by a foreign firm. The building costs will be reflected in the cash account as a *credit* entry, appearing as an increase in Italian holdings of dollars when the American company buys the necessary lire with dollars from an Italian bank.

5. *A $200,000 loan from the U.S. Export–Import Bank to the Indian government for the purchase of American-made machine tools.*

Since the Export–Import Bank is an agency of the U.S. government, the $200,000 loan will appear as a government transaction on capital account. It will be a *debit* because it generates a claim on India. It will also give rise to a *credit* on cash account—an increase in Indian holdings of dollars. When, however, the Indian government draws down its dollar balance to buy machinery, a *credit* entry will appear on current account; an export of machine tools will increase American income but reduce the supply of goods available to Americans. A corresponding *debit* entry will appear on cash account.

Now total up the entries in each section of Table 4–1—the current, capital, and cash accounts. Notice that the balance on current account *plus* the balance on capital account must offset the balance on cash account. The excess of American spending abroad, including purchases of long-term earning assets, must match the net change in the American cash position. The United States is $290,000 richer in goods and earning assets, but poorer in cash by a like amount; it owes $100,000 more to foreign banks and holds $190,000 less of foreign currencies. We shall call this reduction in the U.S. cash position the *gross payments deficit*.[2] It measures the gap between gross payments *from* the United States and gross payments *to* the United States, and is the first of two concepts we will employ to measure imbalances in external payments.

In Table 4–1, the United States has a gross deficit even though it also has a current-account surplus. By implication, a country may have a deficit although it is quite capable of earning its way in world markets. Such a country is merely using cash or credit to acquire extra earning assets. This is precisely what the United States had done during recent years, and it is not necessarily a "bad thing." If a country starts out with a strong cash position, it may do well to run a deficit in order to acquire more earning assets. A deficit becomes dangerous only when it cuts so deeply into cash holdings that a country can no longer cope with unplanned deficits arising from cyclical and other disturbances—or when the deficit continues despite every effort to staunch it, so that citizens and foreigners alike begin to doubt the government's ability to control the situation.

A balance-of-payments table is chiefly designed to measure deficits and surpluses with the outside world, but tells us much more.[3] First, the current account shows how foreign trade affects total income at home and abroad. In our example, Americans have earned $550,000 by selling goods and services to other countries; foreigners have earned $240,000. Second, the cash account shows what has happened to the public's cash holdings at home and abroad. Foreign banks have acquired an additional $100,000 of dollar balances; these funds came from American firms and households. American banks have lost $190,000 worth of foreign currency; these funds were paid to foreigners. Thus, dollar bank deposits held by Americans have fallen by $100,000, while the foreign-currency bank deposits of foreigners have increased by the equivalent of $190,000. Finally, the cash account shows what has happened to the working balances of foreign currencies held by banks. American banks have run down their balances by the equivalent of $190,000; foreign banks have increased theirs by $100,000.

ALTERNATIVE MONETARY SYSTEMS

The banks' working balances of foreign exchange play a strategic role in the international payments system. Each transaction in Table 4–1 drew upon or added to those balances, as the banks stood by to furnish foreign cur-

---

[2] It is sometimes called the "basic" deficit, but we prefer the term used in the text.

[3] In actual practice, however, the accounts are not drawn up like Table 4–1, transaction by transaction. Instead, the satisticians gather the available data on each type of flow (goods, services, direct investment, and long-term securities transactions), then try to reconcile the balance on current and capital account with the separate banking data on cash holdings. They cannot do this perfectly, as many items escape the statisticians' net. Each country's balance-of-payments table, therefore, has a term that Table 4–1 lacked—an allowance for "errors and omissions" to fill the gap between the recorded surplus or deficit and the net change in the cash position. We will look at an actual balance-of-payments table in Chapter 5 and will find some other differences between Table 4–1 and the real thing.

rencies and U.S. dollars when traders and investors needed them. But the banks cannot let their holdings fall very low because they must have foreign currencies on hand to make future sales. Nor can they allow their balances to rise very high because they would tie up loanable funds in their foreign-exchange business and, more importantly, could suffer losses if exchange rates changed. The banks must keep close control over their inventories. Thus, in Table 4–1, foreign banks might seek to sell all or part of the $100,000 increase in their dollar balances, and U.S. banks might seek to purchase foreign currencies in order to make good all or part of the $190,000 decrease.

Suppose, then, that foreign banks seek to sell $50,000 and that U.S. banks seek to buy $130,000 worth of foreign currencies. The foreign banks will offer $50,000 in the New York foreign-exchange market, in exchange for an assortment of pounds, francs, marks, and other currencies. The American banks will enter the same market, offering $130,000 in exchange for a similar assortment. This foreign-exchange market is nothing more than a network of telephone connections among major banks and brokers. But it is much like any other market, where variations in supply and demand lead to price changes. We will, indeed, analyze the foreign-exchange market using supply-and-demand curves.

With foreign and American commercial banks trying to buy $180,000 worth of foreign currencies ($50,000 *plus* $130,000), there will be an *excess demand* for foreign currency (an *excess supply* of dollars) in the foreign-exchange market. Hereafter, this excess demand for foreign currency will be called the *net payments deficit*. It is the best available measure of payments disequilibrium because, unlike the *gross deficit*, it corresponds to the actual excess supply of dollars in the foreign exchange market. Although there was a gross deficit of $290,000 in Table 4–1, the deficit that must be either eliminated or financed is the net deficit that exists in the foreign exchange market.

The appearance of a net deficit will touch off a chain of events that will eventually react on the current and the capital accounts in the balance of payments. They will decrease the American demand for foreign currencies and increase the foreign demand for U.S. dollars. They will thereby reduce the gross payments deficit and restore equilibrium in the foreign-exchange market by forestalling further changes in the banks' working balances. But the nature and the sequence of these happenings will depend on the organization of the international monetary system—on the extent to which exchange rates are free to fluctuate and on the way each country's money supply is connected to its gold and foreign-exchange holdings. To illustrate, we shall describe three monetary systems and show how they would operate if there were an excess demand for foreign currency.

1. *A system of* flexible exchange rates, *under which the prices of foreign currencies are left to fluctuate when there are changes in supply and demand.* Here, exchange-rate changes will operate directly to eliminate any excess demand for foreign currencies. The prices of foreign currencies will rise, making foreign

goods more expensive for Americans and making American goods cheaper for foreigners. Americans will buy fewer foreign goods, and foreigners will buy more American goods.

2. *A* pure gold standard, *under which the prices of foreign currencies cannot change because every currency has a fixed gold value.* If one currency is worth 20 grains of gold and another is worth 10, the first can always be exchanged for 2 units of the second. With an excess demand for foreign currencies, gold will flow out of the United States, reducing its money supply and, therefore, its price level. Entering other countries, it will augment their money supplies and will raise their prices. These price-level changes will work just like exchange-rate changes, making foreign goods more expensive for Americans and making U.S. goods cheaper for foreigners. A gold flow will also alter interest rates and attract short-term capital to the United States.

3. *A system of* managed exchange rates, *under which exchange rates are stabilized by official intervention in the foreign-exchange market.* Here, too, supplies of money may change, altering prices and the balance of payments. But there may be no strict link between the domestic monetary situation and the foreign-exchange market. Hence, price levels will not necessarily change to combat an excess demand for foreign currencies, and governments may then be compelled to alter exchange rates by changing their behavior in the foreign-exchange market. Under a managed rate system, unlike the other systems described, no adjustment forces need be set in motion by the net deficit itself. A government may be able to stabilize the exchange rate without adjusting capital or current account; the system can remain in a state of disequilibrium.

Payments Adjustment under Flexible Exchange Rates

If exchange rates were free to fluctuate, an excess demand for foreign currencies would cause the dollar to *depreciate.* It would depress the price of the dollar in terms of foreign currencies or, what is the same thing, would raise the dollar prices of foreign currencies. This change in exchange rates, in turn, could alter the flow of trade. If the French franc were selling for $0.25 to start, a French car costing 6,000 francs would sell for $1,500. An excess demand for foreign currencies that raised the dollar price of the French franc to $0.40 would raise the dollar price of that French car to $2,400. Americans would buy fewer French cars. Similarly, an American machine costing $10,000 would sell at first for 40,000 francs, but for only 25,000 francs after the depreciation of the dollar. French industry would buy more American machines. These changes in U.S. imports and exports would alter the supply of dollars and the demand for dollars on the foreign-exchange market.

Consider the demand for dollars, analyzed in Fig. 4–1. The vertical axis in Panel A shows the price of an American machine in French francs. The vertical axis in Panel B shows the price of that machine in U.S. dollars. If, for instance,

59

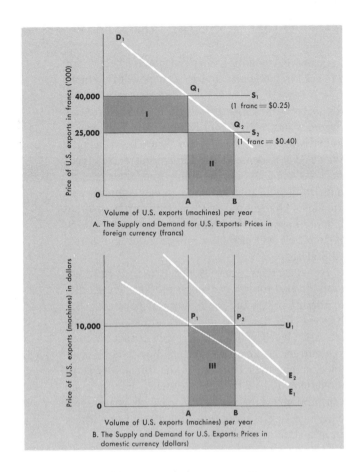

A. The Supply and Demand for U.S. Exports: Prices in foreign currency (francs)

B. The Supply and Demand for U.S. Exports: Prices in domestic currency (dollars)

FIG. 4–1 Currency depreciation and the demand for exports. A depreciation of the dollar lowers the franc price of U.S. machines from S_1 to S_2. It will increase total franc spending on U.S. machines if rectangle I is larger than rectangle II. But it will always increase the French demand for dollars, as dollar spending on U.S. machines will rise by $10,000 × AB (the area of rectangle III).

the dollar price of a machine is $10,000 and a dollar will buy 4 French francs, the French franc price of the machine will be 40,000 francs, as shown in Panel A. The horizontal axes of both panels list export volume (the number of machines), and this must be the same in both parts of the diagram. Finally, Panel A shows the French demand for U.S. machines, the curve D_1, which gives an equilibrium at Q_1. The United States will export OA machines, receiving 40,000 × OA francs.

Now let the dollar depreciate in the foreign-exchange market. The dollar price of an American machine need not change at all (U_1 need not shift). But the franc price of that machine has to fall apace with the depreciation. If, then, the depreciation raises the price of the franc all the way to $0.40, the franc price of a single American machine will drop to 25,000 and the supply curve facing French buyers will be S_2 instead of S_1. Equilibrium will be dispaced to Q_2, and French imports of American machines will rise to OB.

The number of French francs spent on imports of machines may either rise or fall with the depreciation of the U.S. dollar. (It will fall if rectangle I is larger than rectangle II, and will rise if rectangle I is smaller than rectangle II.) But this ambiguity need not concern us, for we want to measure the change in the demand for dollars, not in the supply of francs. Look, then, at Panel B, and notice that the dollar price of a machine has not changed at all, so that the French demand for dollars is bound to rise when the dollar depreciates. The increase in the French demand for U.S. machines appears as a rightward shift in the demand curve (from E_1 to E_2), and the French demand for dollars grows by $10,000 $\times$ AB, equal to the area of rectangle III.

Consider, next, the impact of depreciation on the supply of dollars, analyzed in Fig. 4–2.[4] The vertical axis of this diagram measures the dollar price of

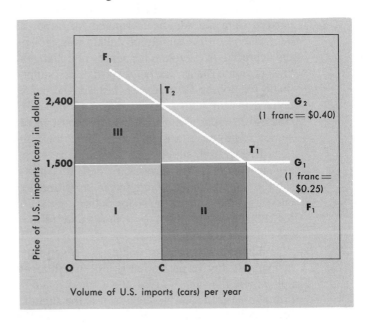

FIG. 4–2 Currency depreciation and the demand for imports. A depreciation of the dollar could raise or lower the supply of dollars on the foreign-exchange market. It will raise the supply if rectangle III is larger than rectangle II. It will lower the supply if rectangle III is smaller than rectangle II.

French cars and the horizontal axis measures the number of cars imported by the United States. If, to start, the supply curve is G_1 and the demand curve is F_1, there will be an equilibrium at T_1. Americans will import OD cars. If, later, the dollar depreciates, raising the price of the franc from $0.25 to $0.40, the dollar price of a French car will rise by 60 per cent, and the supply curve facing American buyers will shift to G_2. Equilibrium will be displaced to T_2, and the volume of imports will decline to OC.

Total American spending on French cars (the supply of dollars) before the depreciation equals the area $OD \times DT_1$ (the sum of rectangles I and II), and after the depreciation the area $OC \times CT_2$ (the sum of rectangles I and III). Total American spending will rise, and the depreciation will increase the supply of dollars, if rectangle III, the extra dollar outlay on cars after depreciation, is

[4]Here we do not need two panels, for Fig. 4–2 by itself will show us the change in dollar supply.   **61**

greater than rectangle II, the decline in dollar outlay due to the lower import volume. If rectangle III is smaller than rectangle II, depreciation will decrease the supply of dollars. The change in total spending on French cars, then, depends on the *elasticity* of F_1F_1, the American demand curve for French cars. If the curve is *elastic*, total spending and the supply of dollars fall when the dollar depreciates to $0.40. If the demand curve is *inelastic*, total spending on cars and the supply of dollars rise as a result of the depreciation.

In Fig. 4–1, where the French demand for dollars was derived from the French demand for American exports, a depreciation unambiguously increased the demand for dollars. In Fig. 4–2, where the American supply of dollars was derived from the American demand for imports from France, the effect of the depreciation on the supply of dollars was shown to be ambiguous. If, however, the depreciation *decreases* the *supply* of dollars, the total effect of the depreciation must decrease the *excess supply* of dollars (supply *minus* demand), since the demand for dollars must rise. If, instead, the depreciation *increases* the supply of dollars, the total effect on *excess supply* depends on the relative sizes of the increases in supply and demand; supply must increase less than demand if depreciation is still to reduce the excess supply of dollars.

In Fig. 4–3, supply and demand curves for *dollars* are plotted against the exchange rate. These curves are derived from Fig. 4–1 and Fig. 4–2, which showed supply and demand for *imports* and *exports* rather than dollars. The curve d_1 is the demand curve for dollars, derived directly from the demand curve for U.S. exports in Fig. 4–1. It shows that, as the dollar depreciates, the demand for dollars must rise.

The supply curve for dollars is derived from F_1F_1, the *demand for imports* in Fig. 4–2, but its derivation is less straightforward. In Fig. 4–2, the supply of dollars was the sum of areas under the demand curve F_1F_1; at the exchange rate of $0.25 (4 francs to the dollar), it is the sum of rectangles I and II. This quantity of dollars is plotted as the distance OM_1 in Fig. 4–3. At the exchange rate of $0.40 (2.5 francs to the dollar), it is the sum of rectangles I and III in Fig. 4–2. This quantity of dollars is plotted as the distance OM_2 in Fig. 4–3. Every other point on S_1 is derived similarly; it is the total supply of dollars generated by the American demand for imports at each exchange rate. The curve S_1 will be backward bending—the supply of dollars will increase as the price of the dollar falls—when the area under the demand curve F_1F_1 increases (when F_1F_1 is inelastic). The curve S_1 will have the more familiar positive slope—the supply of dollars will decrease as the price of the dollar falls—when the area under F_1F_1 decreases (when F_1F_1 is elastic).

Figure 4–3 indicates that in a free market, the supply and demand curves for dollars would intersect at Z_1 and the foreign-exchange market would be in equilibrium at an exchange rate of 4.0 francs to the dollar. If the foreign demand for U.S. exports were to fall, the foreign demand for dollars would also fall, shifting to d_2. At the old exchange rate, there would be an excess supply of dollars, Z_1X

or NM_1 in the foreign-exchange market. This excess supply of dollars is, in fact, the *net payments deficit*. It measures the extent of disequilibrium in the foreign exchange market and the pressure on the exchange rate to depreciate. The needed depreciation will raise the number of dollars demanded by NM_2 and lower the number of dollars supplied by M_1M_2. A new equilibrium will take hold at Z_2, and the excess supply of dollars will disappear.[5]

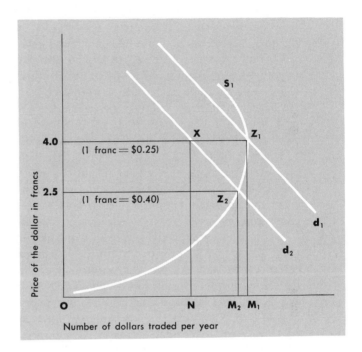

FIG. 4–3 Supply and demand in the foreign-exchange market. A decrease in the demand for dollars (the shift in the demand curve from d_1 to d_2) would cause the dollar to depreciate. Fewer francs would be needed to buy a dollar, and a dollar would buy fewer francs.

The Mechanics of a Pure Gold Standard

The old-fashioned gold standard furnished a simple way to maintain fixed exchange rates and to regulate the quantity of money. Under the gold standard, each government defined its monetary unit (the dollar, pound, franc, and so on) in grains or ounces of gold metal, then stood ready to sell gold for its currency and its currency for gold. Some governments went further, issuing gold coins, but this was not vital. The gold-standard mechanism worked as well when governments issued paper money fully backed by gold, so that any change in central-bank gold holdings forced an equal change in currency outstanding (or in bank reserves).

[5] A depreciation will fail to reduce the excess supply of dollars when, on the backward-bending part of the supply curve, the supply curve cuts the demand curve from above (if the elasticity of supply is less than the elasticity of demand).

There are vestiges of this arrangement in the American monetary system. The United States Treasury still buys gold from foreign governments at $35 per Troy ounce (less a small commission) and sells it at that same price (plus a small commission). The dollar, then is valued at 1/35 of an ounce of gold. Furthermore, the Federal Reserve Banks hold gold certificates, which give them title to Treasury gold. But the United States does not sell gold to individuals, here or abroad. Nor is there any direct link between the U.S. gold stock and the supply of money in the United States. The Federal Reserve Banks can increase their liabilities (currency and bank reserves) by buying government securities in the open market, without also taking on more gold.

If all currencies were pegged to gold, and governments were willing to deal in gold with private citizens as well as with other governments, an *implicit* exchange rate would be established between each pair of currencies. If, for example, the French franc were freely exchangeable for gold at 140 francs per ounce of gold, it would exchange for $0.25 in American currency; 140 francs would buy an ounce of gold and an ounce of gold would buy $35. Hence, 140 francs = $35, and 1 franc = $35/140 = $0.25. The actual exchange rates could still fluctuate a bit, since governments might charge small commissions and bankers would have to pay the cost of shipping gold from one country to another. But when an exchange rate ran outside the boundaries set by these commissions and costs, someone could profit by engaging in *arbitrage*.

An *arbitrageur* would buy gold with the currency that was at a discount (sold at less than its gold parity) in the foreign-exchange market, sell it for the currency that was at a premium (sold at more than its gold parity), then sell the second currency for the first. Suppose that the franc rose from $0.25 to $0.28 and that it cost $0.10 in commissions, insurance and freight to ship an ounce of gold from New York to Paris. An *arbitrageur* could buy a thousand ounces of gold from the United States Treasury and ship them to Paris at a total cost of $35,100 ($35,000 for the gold and $100 in other costs). He could then sell the thousand ounces of gold to the Bank of France for 140,000 francs. Finally, he could sell these francs for dollars in the foreign-exchange market and would receive $0.28 × 140,000 = $39,200. His profit would be $39,200 *minus* $35,100 = $4,100. He could make nearly 12 per cent on his capital in a matter of days! The *arbitrageur,* moreover, would also help to raise the price of the dollar when he bought dollars with francs at the end of his three-part transaction. Arbitrage would serve to keep the actual exchange rate close to the ratio of gold parities.

These transactions would show up in our supply–and–demand diagram of the foreign-exchange market (Fig. 4–3). With a flexible exchange rate, a shift in the demand for dollars was met by a change in the price of the dollar; when the demand curve in Fig. 4–3 dropped from d_1 to d_2, the exchange rate changed from 4.0 to 2.5 francs per U.S. dollar. With a pure gold standard, a shift in the demand curve would push the dollar to a discount, make arbitrage profitable, and cause a gold outflow. The gold outflow would create a demand for dollars and prevent the exchange rate from depreciating. We saw that when the exchange rate is \$0.25, the excess supply of dollars is XZ_1; to prevent depreciation, therefore, the gold outflow induced by arbitrage must create a demand for dollars equal to XZ_1, and the size of the gold outflow necessary to stabilize the exchange rate at \$0.25 is likewise XZ_1 dollars worth of gold. If less than XZ_1 gold flowed out, the dollar would begin to depreciate, thereby stimulating the needed additional arbitrage and the corresponding gold outflow.

We have already identified XZ_1 as the *net payments deficit*. Note, now, that the gold outflow under a pure gold standard will equal the net payments deficit; gold flows "finance" the deficit and serve also to measure the extent of the balance-of-payments disequilibrium. More importantly, under a pure gold standard, gold flows trigger major changes in the money supplies of the deficit and surplus countries. The country in *net deficit* will suffer a decline in its money supply, while the country in *net surplus* will experience an increase. These monetary changes are direct results of the gold movements that finance and measure net deficits and surpluses. They are unavoidable under a gold standard, as the central banks cannot offset them by open-market operations. In consequence, a pure gold standard is guaranteed to combat disequilibria.

Adjustment Process Under the Pure Gold Standard

To trace the process of adjustment under a gold standard, look at Table 4–2. The adjustment begins when an arbitrageur or broker buys \$180,000 (the size of the net deficit) worth of gold from the Treasury. The Treasury deposits the broker's check at the Federal Reserve Bank of New York, enlarging its balance there and replacing one monetary asset (gold) with another (a bank deposit). The Federal Reserve Bank sends the broker's check to the commercial bank on which it was drawn, and deducts \$180,000 from that bank's deposit balance, reducing one of its deposit liabilities to offset the increase in another. The commercial bank can also balance its books. It deducts \$180,000 from the

Table 4–2   GOLD FLOWS AND THE U.S. MONEY SUPPLY:

CHANGES IN TREASURY, FEDERAL RESERVE, AND

COMMERCIAL-BANK BALANCE SHEETS (thousands of dollars)

Institution and Item	Asset	Liability
U.S. Treasury		
Gold stock	−180	—
Balance at Federal Reserve Bank	+180	—
Federal Reserve Bank of New York		
Treasury deposit balance	—	+180
Member-bank deposit balance	—	−180
Commercial Bank		
Member-bank deposit balance	−180	—
Broker's deposit balance	—	−180

broker's own account when the broker's check arrives, reducing its total liabilities to offset the decline in its assets.

When these transactions are complete, everyone has balanced books. But the process of monetary contraction is far from finished. If the commercial banks were "loaned up" before the gold loss (if they had no excess reserves), they must now cut down their lending and deposits. Suppose they must maintain a 10 per cent reserve against demand deposits. They will have to reduce their deposit obligations by a full $1,800,000, because they have lost $180,000 in reserve balances. To do so, they must cut back their loans or investments by $1,620,000. When this process (summarized in Table 4–3) is completed, the $180,000 gold loss will have reduced the money supply by $1,800,000.

Similar transactions will occur in France, but will run the other way. When the broker sells his gold to the Bank of France, he will receive a check drawn on the Bank of France. He must sell that check to move back into dollars, but the foreign-exchange dealer buying it from him will, in turn, deposit it with a French commercial bank. That bank will send the check back to the Bank of France and will receive extra reserves. French banks will be able to expand their lending and the French money supply.

Monetary changes such as these will affect interest rates in the United States and France, altering the current and capital accounts. A decrease in the U.S. money supply will raise U.S. interest rates; an increase in the French money supply will reduce French interest rates. Short-term capital will flow to the United States in search of higher yields, augmenting the demand for dollars in the foreign-exchange market. Domestic spending will decline in the United States and will rise in France, causing wage and price changes that have the same effects as an exchange-rate change.

Table 4–3   GOLD FLOWS AND THE U.S. MONEY SUPPLY:

MEMORANDUM ON COMMERCIAL-BANK RESERVES (thousands of dollars)

Initial decrease in deposit liabilities		180
Decrease in total reserves (member-bank balances)	180	
Decrease in required reserves (10 per cent reserve requirement against demand deposits)	18	
Reserve deficiency	162	
Secondary decrease in lending and deposits (due to deficiency)		1,620
Total decrease in deposit liabilities		1,800

Interest rates and capital movements. An increase in U.S. interest rates relative to foreign rates can generate several types of short-term lending and investment. First, it may alter the financing of foreign trade. An American importer who usually borrows dollars from a New York bank and converts them to sterling to pay for British goods may, instead, borrow sterling directly from a London bank. A British importer who ordinarily borrows dollars in New York may, instead, borrow sterling in London, then swap it for dollars to pay for his purchases. American importers who borrow in London reduce the supply of dollars in the exchange market. British importers who borrow in London increase the demand for dollars. Hence, changes in the *locus* of commercial borrowing will help to reduce the excess supply of dollars. Next, a change in interest rates can foster explicit cash transfers. A British corporation that normally invests its idle funds in British Treasury bills may send its money to New York to buy U.S. Treasury bills or other money-market instruments. An American corporation that normally holds money in London to finance its foreign operations may transfer cash to New York to earn a higher interest rate. These two transfers will also increase the demand for dollars.

But short-term capital flows can aid the dollar only temporarily; money borrowed today must be repaid in a few months. Furthermore, there is a built-in market mechanism working to arrest transfers of funds. When American importers borrow in London and British firms place cash in New York, they run the risk that the dollar will depreciate. Were this to happen, Americans would have to spend more dollars to repay their sterling debts, and British companies would get fewer pounds for the dollars they invested in New York.[6] To protect themselves against this exchange risk, investors and borrowers can arrange *forward* foreign-exchange contracts. A British company with cash invested in New York can contract to deliver at some future date for a specified number of pounds the dollars earned on its investment. Similarly, an American importer with a fixed sterling debt can contract to receive the necessary number of pounds at a future date with the exchange rate fixed now. These contracts are made on the *forward market*, at the *forward exchange rate*. (The exchange rates discussed until now have been *spot rates*.) Forward rates, however, may be quite different from the spot rates at which currencies are traded for immediate delivery. Thus a British investor in New York would incur extra costs if the forward pound were at a premium (if the forward rate were above the spot rate), for he would receive fewer pounds for a given amount of dollars.

Furthermore, the forward rate *will* in fact tend to move in sympathy with the interest-rate difference between New York and London, increasing the cost of investing in New York. When interest rates are higher in New York than in London, the pound tends toward a premium in the forward market (see Fig. 4–4). This is because importers borrowing in London and companies investing in New York are buying forward sterling to *hedge* against exchange risks— thereby augmenting the demand for forward sterling, thereby raising forward sterling to a premium and reducing the incentive to invest in New York.

To sum up, an interest-rate difference caused by changes in money supplies can help to remove a payments deficit, but can rarely do the whole job. A more

---

[6]This risk is much greater with managed exchange rates than with a pure gold standard. But it also existed in the heyday of the gold standard, before 1914. Exchange rates could still move within the so-called "gold points," and the gold parities could change.

lasting change is needed to remove an excess supply of dollars. The gold standard has also to alter costs and prices.

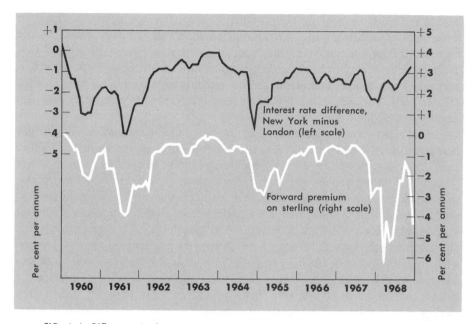

FIG. 4–4 Differences in short-term rates and the premium on forward foreign exchange. When New York interest rates are above London interest rates, the pound rises to a premium in the forward foreign-exchange market. When London interest rates are above New York rates, the pound falls to a discount. The relationship is even closer than the chart indicates; the right scale has been lowered to disentagle the two lines. (Source: Board of Governors of the Federal Reserve System, *Federal Reserve Bulletin*, various issues.)

Interest rates, spending, and prices. Early economic theory connected money and prices by a simple axiom: If the supply of money falls, prices have to fall, so that the remaining currency can do its work efficiently. Early writers on international finance consequently argued that a gold standard would be self-adjusting. A gold transfer from Britain to France would reduce British prices and raise French prices; the citizens of both countries would buy more British goods and fewer French goods; Britain would develop a surplus on current account; gold would flow back to Britain. David Hume, the eighteenth-century philosopher, put this *specie-flow doctrine* very neatly:

> Suppose four-fifths of all the money in Great Britain to be annihilated in one night, and the nation reduced to the same condition, with regard to specie, as in the reigns of the Harrys and Edwards, what would be the consequence? Must not the price of all labour and commodities sink in proportion, and everything be sold as cheap as they were in those ages? What nation could then dispute with us in any foreign market, or pretend to navigate or to sell

manufacturers at the same price, which to us would afford sufficient profit? In how little time, therefore, must this bring back the money which we had lost, and raise us to the level of all the neighboring nations? Where, after we have arrived, we immediately lose the advantage of the cheapness of labour and commodities; and the farther flowing in of money is stopped by our fulness and repletion.

But even if wages and prices moved smoothly, the connection between money and prices would be less direct than Hume implied. Most economists would first link the supply of money to the rate of interest, then link the interest rate to total spending, spending to employment, and employment to wage rates. Only then would they come to prices.

A fall in the quantity of money will increase the interest rate because it is accomplished by reductions in bank lending—in the supply of loanable funds— and a cut in the supply of credit will raise its price. When interest rates increase, however, aggregate spending is apt to fall. Some forms of business investment are sensitive to changes in interest rates or to the credit rationing that comes with higher interest rates. Reductions in investment, moreover, depress every form of private spending; a *multiplier* process is set to work, reducing consumption along with investment. Finally, a reduction in aggregate spending will depress output and employment, and the consequent increase in unemployment will cause workers to bid down money wage rates, cutting costs and prices.

From here on, the argument is much like Hume's own exposition, with one qualification. A reduction in the prices of the country losing gold relative to those of the country gaining gold will increase the exports of the deficit country and re- duce its imports. This will improve its balance of payments and stem its gold loss, provided the changes in the volume of trade are larger than the changes in prices. But just as one expects exchange depreciation to improve a country's balance of payments, so one would expect deflation to do so. The gold-standard mechanism and exchange-rate changes have similar effect if wage rates are flexible. The chief difference between them is that an exchange-rate change moves one vital price, whereas the gold standard keeps that one price constant and moves all the rest.

Payments Adjustment under Managed Exchange Rates

Although the United States pegs its currency to gold, we do not have a pure gold standard. As the Federal Reserve Banks can hold other assets (government securities) against their liabilities (currency and member-bank deposits), there is no strict link between gold movements and the American money supply. Furthermore, other currencies are not pegged to gold, so that there is no implicit exchange rate between the dollar and those currencies. Yet most countries do maintain stable exchange rates by direct action. Instead of holding gold as "back- ing" for their currencies and passively awaiting gold-market arbitrage, they have established exchange stabilization funds under central bank or treasury control. **69** These funds hold gold and foreign currencies and use these reserves to finance intervention in the foreign-exchange markets. When the price of a country's currency rises, its exchange stabilization fund sells domestic currency for foreign currencies, reducing the price. It adds the foreign currencies to its portfolio. When the price of the domestic currency falls, the exchange stabilization fund buys that currency with foreign currencies, raising the price. It takes the foreign currency out of its reserves. In Fig. 4–3, for example, the Bank of France might buy up Z_1X dollars, the excess supply, to keep the exchange rate stable at four francs to the dollar. It would put French francs into the market and take out dollars. The Bank of France could retain the dollars it had bought, or could convert them into gold at the U.S. Treasury. The Bank of France need not act as soon as the exchange rate starts to change, but under the rules of the International Monetary Fund, it must intervene whenever the exchange rate moves by as much as 1 per cent from its established parity. This 1 per cent margin is akin to the range that existed under the gold standard.

Once again, the excess supply of dollars, Z_1X_1, purchased by the Bank of France, equals the *net payments* deficit. Under the managed exchange-rate system, however, this statistic measures the extent of official intervention necessary to maintain the exchange parity and is commonly called the *deficit measured by official settlements*. In Table 4–4 we can follow the relationship between this deficit and the gross payments deficit. Recall that the gross deficit in Table 4–1 was $290,000, equal to the increase in foreign holdings of dollars of $100,000 and the decrease in U.S. holdings of foreign currencies of $190,000. However, the net deficit was $180,000, as foreign banks decided to hold $50,000, and sell $50,000, while U.S. banks bought $130,000 of foreign currencies and let their inventories fall by $60,000. Thus $110,000 of the gross deficit was financed by changes in *private* holdings and claims (the additional $50,000 held by foreign banks and the $60,000 decrease in foreign currencies absorbed by U.S. banks). This is shown in the upper part of Table 4–4. The remaining $180,000, the net deficit, must be met by changes in official holdings and claims.

If the Bank of France decided to retain all the dollars acquired by market intervention, Table 4–4 would show foreign official dollar holdings rising by $180,000.

Table 4–4   THE CASH ACCOUNT AND THE OFFICIAL SETTLEMENTS

DEFICIT (thousands of dollars)

Cash Account (gross deficit)	+290
Private Holdings	+110
Increase (+) in foreign holdings of dollars	+ 50
Increase (—) in U.S. holdings of foreign currency	+ 60
Official Settlements (net deficit)	+180
Foreign official dollar holdings [increase (+)]	+ 40
Increase (—) in U.S. gold stock	+140

If the Bank of France decided to buy $140,000 of gold from the United States Treasury, retaining only $40,000 in dollar balances, the transactions would match those shown in Table 4–4.[7]

If the Bank of France does buy gold, the American money supply will fall, as in Tables 4–2 and 4–3. If it holds onto the dollars, there may still be a decline in the money supply, but the process will differ from that of the gold standard. Many central banks keep their dollars on deposit with the Federal Reserve Banks. To do so, the Bank of France will draw a check on the New York commercial bank where its dollars lay when it acquired them from the foreign-exchange dealer. It will send that check to the Federal Reserve Bank of New York, which will credit the Bank of France with $180,000 and deduct the same amount from the deposit account of the commercial bank. The commercial bank's reserves will fall by $180,000, and it will have to cut back its loans or investments. There will also be an increase in the French money supply. When the Bank of France buys dollars from the foreign-exchange market, it creates new French francs, and these will find their way into the reserves of the French commercial banks.

Table 4–5   U.S. GOLD STOCK AND COMMERCIAL-BANK RESERVE BALANCES AT THE FEDERAL RESERVE BANKS

(millions of dollars)

Item	1939–1941	1961–1963
Change in U.S. gold stock	+5,241	−4,367
Change in foreign deposits at the Federal Reserve Banks	+ 792*	− 69
Net foreign influence (gold *less* deposits)	+4,449	−4,298
Federal Reserve credit, currency in circulation, and Treasury operations	−3,108	+4,342
Total (equals change in commercial-bank reserve balances at the Federal Reserve Banks)	+1,341	+ 44

*Includes the change in "other" domestic deposits that could not be separated from foreign accounts.

Source: Board of Governors of the Federal Reserve System, *Federal Reserve Bulletin.*

If this were all that happened under managed exchange rates, the system would resemble a pure gold standard. There would be an increase in U.S. interest rates and a drop in French rates. Short-term capital would flow to the

[7]Thus, the size of U.S. gold losses depends on the size of the U.S. payments deficits *and* on the reserve-asset preferences of foreign central banks. If the United States runs a payments deficit *vis-à-vis* countries whose central banks usually hold onto the dollars they acquire, the U.S. payments deficit need not cause a gold loss. If it runs a deficit *vis-à-vis* countries whose central banks normally hold gold, like Britain, France, and Switzerland, it will almost always lose some gold. The United States can also lose gold without having a deficit. This may happen when a dollar-holding country runs a deficit with a gold-holding country, transferring dollar deposits to a central bank that will use them to buy gold. It can also lose gold when a foreign central bank alters its portfolio of reserve assets. One such instance occurred in 1964–1965, when France cashed in $1 billion of dollar reserves.

United States and prices would begin to change, altering trade flows and stemming the deficit. But something else can happen with managed exchange rates. The central banks may not allow money supplies to change. The Federal Reserve Banks may buy government securities in the open market to replenish American bank reserves, forestalling a contraction in loans and deposits. The Bank of France may sell government securities to reduce French bank reserves, forestalling an increase in loans and deposits.[8]

Central banks are prone to follow these policies—to "neutralize" gold flows. Look at Table 4–5 to see two such episodes. In 1939–1941, the U.S. gold stock rose by $5.2 billion. Part of this increase was allowed to augment bank reserves, but most of it was offset by open-market operations. In 1961–1963, the U.S. gold stock fell by $4.4 billion, but the entire change was offset by domestic operations.

DOMESTIC AND EXTERNAL EQUILIBRIUM

Why should central banks offset external disturbances when, by doing so, they interfere with the restoration of payments equilibrium? Why have the Federal Reserve Banks neutralized U.S. gold losses in the 1960's, allowing the United States to go on running a payments deficit?

The answer is quite simple. To achieve an external equilibrium by domestic deflation is very much more painful than we have indicated heretofore. Wage rates and prices do not fall easily, and a decline in total spending brought about by higher interest rates (or by fiscal policy) will lead to unemployment, not to wage reductions. If the United States sought to reach external balance by following the gold-standard rules, it would have to sacrifice full employment. Its imports would still shrink as domestic spending fell. But the decline in its imports would be caused by a reduction in its real income, not by a reduction in prices. Furthermore, a balance-of-payments deficit can sometimes depress employment directly, and governments are loath to compound this direct effect. They may even try to combat it.

National Income and Foreign Trade

To understand the links between exports, imports, and employment when wages are rigid, you must start with the basic income identities.[9] In an open economy (one with foreign trade), three types of spending contribute to the national income:

---

[8]Central banks can also change the reserve requirement under which the commercial banks operate. The Federal Reserve System can reduce the U.S. reserve ratio; the Bank of France can raise the French reserve ratio. They can thereby align reserve requirements with the actual changes in reserves.

[9]This analysis ignores the role of government expenditure, as its inclusion would complicate the analysis without changing the result.

C Consumption (household spending)
I Investment (business spending)
X Exports (foreign spending)

But each of these three streams includes spending on imported goods as well as domestic products; even exports may include imported raw materials. One must therefore deduct imports, M, from total spending in order to define domestic income, Y:

$$C + I + X - M = Y$$

This accounting relationship tells only half the story. To complete it, one has now to note that some of the spending streams listed in the basic income equation are themselves affected by the levels of income.

Consumption, exports, and imports depend quite directly on national income. Given an extra dollar of income, consumers will usually spend part of it on goods and services. This connection is a basic building block of economic analysis. Imports and exports depend on prices and exchange rates, but also respond to changes in income. Imports will increase along with income at home. Exports will increase with income abroad (being the imports of other countries). If, indeed, prices and exchange rates are stable, the connection between income and imports will be much like the link between income and consumption. Part of any increase in income will be spent on imports.

The remaining component of income, business investment, depends on many things, and income may be one of them. But we will suppose that investment is governed by the rate of interest—that it will rise when interest rates fall, and will fall when interest rates rise. On this assumption, monetary policy will affect national income by affecting investment.

The two-way relationship between trade and income gives rise to an important balancing mechanism. Suppose that a change in foreign tastes causes a decline in exports. This decline will produce a payments deficit, but will also cut back national income. The reduction in income will then reduce spending on imports, narrowing the payments deficit. And income will fall more than exports because the decline in income will include a decline in consumption. There is a formal relationship between the export decline and the changes in income and imports. Let the symbol d mean "the change in" so that dY is "the change in income." The change in income must then equal the sum of the change in its components given in the accounting relationship:

$$dY = dC + dI + dX - dM$$

The change in consumption, however, is related to the change in income; the increase in consumption from an extra dollar of income, c, is the *marginal propensity to consume*. Thus:

73

$$c = dC/dY$$
$$\text{or}$$
$$dC = cdY$$

An analogous relationship exists between income and imports. Define the *marginal propensity to import*, *m*, as the increase in imports for a dollar increase in income:

$$m = dM/dY$$
$$\text{or}$$
$$dM = mdY$$

We now have the relationships needed to estimate the decrease in income stemming from a fall in exports. In the accounting equation for dY, substitute our new expressions for dC and dM:

$$dY = cdY + dI + dX - mdY$$

Rearrange terms:

$$dY - cdY + mdY = dI + dX$$
$$\text{and}$$
$$dY(1 - c + m) = dI + dX$$
$$\text{or}$$
$$dY = \frac{dI + dX}{1 - c + m}$$

It is useful to rewrite the denominator of the right-hand side. A dollar of income received must be consumed or saved. Hence one can define the *marginal propensity to save*, *s*, by:

$$s = 1 - c$$

Substituting *s* for $1 - c$ into our final equation for dY, we have the *foreign-trade multiplier*:

$$dY = \frac{dI + dX}{s + m}$$

The change in income, dY, equals $\dfrac{1}{s + m}$ times the initial change in investment or export. Note that the presence of the import leakage, *m*, reduces the change in income below what would occur in a closed economy. In a closed economy, equilibrium occurs when investment and saving are brought into equality. In an open economy, equilibrium requires that investment *plus* exports equal saving *plus* imports. Note, further, that a fall in exports will not be matched by an equal decline in imports. As saving also changes with income, imports will not fall far enough completely to offset the decline in exports.

To illustrate, let $s = 0.1$, $m = 0.4$ and $dX = 100$ (let investment be unchanged, so $dI = 0$). Then $dY = \dfrac{100}{0.1 + 0.4} = 200$. The induced change in imports, $dM = mdY$, is $0.4 \times 200 = 80$; the induced change in saving, $dS = sdY$, is $0.1 \times 200 = 20$. Saving plus imports have changed by 100, matching the change in exports, but imports have changed by only 80, leaving a trade surplus or deficit of 20, depending on the sign of dX. To restore payments equilibrium, the government must foster a further change in income. With a decline in exports, it must let the resulting payments deficit cut into the money supply, and may even have to hasten the contraction by open-market operations. It must end the deficit before it has eaten up the country's reserves of gold and foreign exchange. Monetary contraction will raise interest rates, depress domestic investment, and thereby reduce income and imports. Thus, a fall in investment of 25, reducing income by $\dfrac{25}{0.1 + 0.4} = 50$ and reducing imports by $0.4 \times 50 = 20$ is needed to completely offset a 100 decline in exports.

Clearly, payments equilibrium can be restored only at considerable cost. In order to remove an initial deficit of 100, two doses of deflation were needed (the initial, autonomous decline in exports and the cut in domestic investment induced by monetary contraction). Income has declined by 250, generating unemployment. Rigid wages make deflation a painful way to maintain external balance, and governments are often tempted to offset the automatic monetary processes, rather than to reinforce them. Most countries are unwilling to allow the balance-of-payments tail to wag the national-income dog.

Our income analysis also shows how balance-of-payments problems may strike at a growing economy. Higher incomes spill over into higher imports and growth may have to be restrained if exports do not rise rapidly enough to offset the rise in imports. The ideal situation, from an international point of view, is simultaneous growth in many countries, each providing a demand for the others' products, so that trade can balance at growing income levels.

Modifying Fixed Exchange Rates

Governments faced with payments imbalances and unwilling to permit domestic deflation confront a painful dilemma. With deflation ruled out, they may sometimes be compelled to use the other standard remedy for a payments deficit, *devaluation*.[10] Deflation alters the foreign-currency equivalent of domestic prices by moving one central price, the exchange rate; whereas deflation must

---

[10]We shall henceforth use the term *devaluation* when we mean a once-over change in a fixed exchange rate (accomplished by changing a gold parity or the price at which the central bank intervenes in the foreign-exchange market). We shall use the term *depreciation* when we mean a change in a flexible exchange rate (accomplished by the market forces of supply and demand).

lower all internal prices if it is not to produce painful unemployment. Our analysis of flexible exchange rates showed that devaluation will improve the U.S. balance of payments if import and export demand elasticities are high enough to decrease the excess supply of dollars, and actual demand elasticities are thought to be sufficiently high for this to occur.

Yet governments are usually reluctant to devalue, and when they do, the results are often discouraging. The apparent contradiction can be explained by looking again at the national-income accounting identity. Rewrite it as:

$$X - M = Y - (C + I)$$

Call $C + I$ *expenditure*, E, and $(X - M)$ the *trade balance*, B. Hence:

$$B = Y - E$$

The balance of trade equals the difference between aggregate *output* and aggregate *expenditure*. Suppose, now, that devaluation successfully shifts foreign demand toward domestic goods and shifts domestic demand away from foreign goods. In order to accommodate these demand shifts, the margin between output and expenditure must grow.

If domestic resources are unemployed, B can rise without reducing E; there can be an increase in Y. Previously unemployed resources can produce the requisite addition to exports and the domestic substitutes for imports. When there is *full employment*, however, output cannot rise. A successful devaluation then requires a *fall in expenditure* to release resources for the trade balance. Because domestic output is at its limit, increased exports must use resources previously devoted to serving the home market. Reduced domestic spending on foreign goods cannot be replaced with increased spending on domestic substitutes. The painful lesson is that, with full employment, a devaluation must be accompanied by government measures to reduce domestic spending. Otherwise, the increase of demand for domestic goods—for exports and import substitutes—will drive up domestic prices and wipe out the price advantage conferred by the devaluation. When, too frequently, devaluations fail, it is because governments are unable to resist inflationary pressures.[11]

With deflation usually ruled out, and devaluation resorted to only *in extremis*, governments with payments deficits gloomily contemplate their limited policy options. To raise domestic interest rates, attracting foreign capital, is a frequent expedient, but is, as we saw earlier, self-limiting. Furthermore, it cannot solve a persistent deficit; it can merely buy the time required for other adjustment policies to be put in place and take effect. Governments may also use a panoply of direct controls over foreign trade and capital movements. But these run afoul of international agreements and impair economic efficiency.

[11]The difficulties of devaluation sometimes prompt its critics to call for import controls—tariffs and quotas—instead. This is a non sequitur: import controls that improve the balance of payments have also to be reinforced by measures that reduce domestic consumption and investment.

The fixed exchange-rate system lacks any automatic or efficient machinery to accomplish enduring adjustment. Trade and capital controls distort resource allocation, whereas devaluation and deflation are usually too painful to consider.

Adjustment, however, often occurs, slowly but surely, even inadvertently, because of differential rates of inflation. Inflation is usually inversely related to the level of unemployment, and a deficit country unwilling to accept severe deflation will probably tolerate an unemployment rate higher than otherwise desired. A surplus country, by contrast, may choose to run closer to full employment and will tolerate a higher rate of inflation. Prices will tend to rise more slowly in the deficit country, gradually improving its competitive position. Adjustment, moreover, can be imbedded in global economic growth. A growing economy can alter its costs even though its wage rates are rigid. It can also alter national expenditure without creating massive unemployment. It can seek to tamper with the rates of increase in wages and expenditure, not with the absolute levels.

Suppose, first, that labor productivity is rising steadily in all countries. If a deficit country can hold its wage rates constant, while foreign wages rise apace with productivity, costs and prices will decline in the deficit country, and its balance of payments will improve without any absolute loss of output or employment.

Suppose, next, that output and money incomes are growing together in all countries, so that prices do not change. If a deficit country can keep its domestic expenditure from rising apace with output, it will be able to hold down its imports and enlarge its export capacity. It will experience a gradual improvement in its balance of payments.

But all these indirect effects, though they have a cumulative impact, work very slowly. Payments deficits and surpluses may therefore endure for quite a while, straining international financial arrangements.

International Coordination of Economic Policy

The vicissitudes of life under fixed exchange rates point to the advantages of coordinating national economic policies. At the very least, they warn against policies that operate at cross purposes. Both the United States and Great Britain could raise their interest rates in order to attract short-term capital. Since it is the interest rate differential that matters, however, each country will end up with excessive interest rates, depressing national income, yet achieve no improvement in its balance of payments. To cite a more dramatic example discussed in the next chapter, governments engaged in competitive devaluations during the 1930's, each one wiping out the gains of the one before.

The British devaluation of November 1967 was undertaken in consultation with the other major industrial nations, and was limited in size to avoid endangering other currencies. The French devaluation of August 1969, although undertaken without consultation, was also a "small" devaluation. Some intentional coordination of interest rate policy has also occurred. But these remain isolated examples, and more significant instances of coordination are unlikely in the near future. Adequate coordination would require that internal economic measures, monetary and fiscal, be undertaken for the sake of international adjustment, and nations are as yet unwilling to surrender this much sovereignty.

SUMMARY

Foreign economic policy has two major dimensions. An open economy must formulate *commercial* policies to reap the gains from foreign trade and foreign investment. It must formulate *financial* policies to maintain a monetary equilibrium in its foreign transactions.

The choice among exchange-rate regimes is the first step in making international financial policy. With exchange rates free to fluctuate as market forces dictate, a difference between foreign payments and receipts will appear as excess supply or demand in the foreign-exchange market. An excess supply of domestic currency will cause its price to decline (depreciate); an excess demand will cause it to increase (appreciate). A change in the exchange rate will alter the foreign prices of a country's exports and the domestic prices of its imports. It will have the same effect as a change in a country's over-all price level. A depreciation or deflation will increase the foreign and domestic demand for home goods (shifting demand away from foreign goods) and will restore equilibrium in the foreign-exchange market.

With exchange rates fixed by a gold standard or official intervention in the foreign-exchange markets, an excess supply of home currency will cause a contraction in the domestic money supply and a corresponding expansion abroad. These monetary changes will also re-establish equilibrium, though differently from flexible exchange-rates. They will raise interest rates in the deficit country and depress them in the surplus country. These changes in interest rates will call forth capital flows and will cause price changes affecting the current account.

With rigid costs and prices, however, adjustment must take place through income changes. Some of these changes will occur automatically; a decrease in exports will reduce national income, cutting domestic expenditure on home goods and imports. Some of the changes are indirect, brought on by monetary policy. Higher interest rates in a deficit country will depress investment, reducing income and imports. These indirect effects will continue to operate until the deficit is ended. The money supply will go on shrinking, interest rates will go on rising, and investment will continue to fall, reducing income and imports. With fixed exchange-rates and rigid wage rates, however, governments may face an intractable policy conflict. They may have to choose between full employment and payments equilibrium.

CHAPTER FIVE

THE CHOICE AMONG
EXCHANGE-RATE REGIMES

The world's monetary system most nearly resembled a gold standard during the 40 years before the First World War. By the mid-1870's, each major country had connected its currency to gold, establishing a system of fixed exchange rates that was not altered until 1914. And after the completion of the Atlantic Cable, linking London and New York, the market exchange rates stayed close to their gold parities.

Governments did not give up all of their control over the supply of money. They did not base their currencies wholly on gold. In the United States, for example, banks could issue paper money backed by holdings of government securities. In Britain, the Bank of England bought and sold commercial bills and government securities to ease or tighten credit. But Britain and some other countries adhered to the "rules of the game"; they used monetary policy to reinforce rather than offset the impact of gold flows.

Yet the international payments system did not work quite as theory said it should. The major countries sometimes corrected their payments positions by altering output and employment rather than prices. They sometimes shifted the burden of adjustment onto countries at the periphery of the world economy—the raw-materials producers of the Western Hemisphere and other outlying areas. A tightening of credit in Britain bore heavily on trade in raw materials because this trade was financed with money lent by London. When British interest rates were high and credit scarce in London, dealers in raw materials had to compress their inventories. Doing so, they depressed the prices of raw materials and reduced Britain's import bill. The countries at the periphery, moreover, changed their exchange rates rather often, dropping away from the gold standard during payments crises, and returning at different gold parities.

After the First World War had wrecked the monetary system, the statesmen tried to build a new gold standard. Unfortunately, this attempt ignored the major differences between prewar theory and prewar practice and was therefore doomed to fail. But it might have failed even if its builders had understood the prewar system, for the economic environment had changed. First, there was less flexibility in the international economy—you have already read of the growth in debts, the increase in tariffs, the wide use of quotas, and the huge expansion in farm output. Second, there was less strength at the center of the international financial system—Britain's chief exports, textiles and coal, were meeting fierce competition in foreign markets, while New York and Paris had become major purveyors of capital and credit, so that London could no longer influence international credit conditions as it had before the war. Third, there was less tolerance of unemployment—new political parties drawing support from urban workers threatened any government that dared to cure its payments problems by deflation. Governments, moreover, had found new ways to insulate the national economy from international monetary changes. New central banks had been established in several countries, including the Federal Reserve System in the United States, and all central banks had found new ways to contravene the "rules of the game." Finally, the composition of international reserves had changed. Many countries were holding dollars and sterling, as well as gold. Sterling was the more important of the new reserve-assets; some countries, indeed, invested the bulk of their reserves in London. Even the Bank of France, a pillar of monetary orthodoxy, built up large sterling claims in the 1920's. The new system, then, was a *gold-exchange standard,* not a simple gold standard.

This substitution of currencies for gold was, in part, inspired by fears of a gold shortage and was sanctioned by international financial conferences. But it proved to be a major weakness. Britain had become a banker to other governments and was continually threatened by a run on its own small gold reserves— just like any other banker with no central bank to serve him as lender of last resort. The run finally came in 1931, and dealt the new system its death blow. In 1925, Britain had pegged the pound at its old gold parity, taking no account of the increase in British prices or the weakness of Britain's export industries. As a result, the United States and France ran very large payments surpluses. The United States succeeded in masking its surplus by heavy long-term lending to other countries—huge private purchases of newly issued foreign bonds. France took in gold and built up its sterling claims. With the collapse of the American economy, however, American lending came to a halt. In 1928 there had been a net capital outflow of $1,541,000,000. In 1931 there was a net *inflow* of $756,000,000, and new U.S. purchases of foreign securities were not even large enough to cover redemptions, let alone the massive repatriation of other American capital. At this same critical moment, moreover, the Bank of France began to convert its sterling into gold, putting heavy pressure on the pound. Britain was compelled to abandon the new gold standard in the summer of 1931, when a panic that had started with the collapse of the *Credit Anstalt,* the Rothschild bank in Vienna, spread across Europe and began to lap at Britain's gold reserves.

The 1930's saw complete monetary chaos. Many small countries had left the gold standard in 1929 and 1930; others followed in 1931 and 1932. Their currencies fluctuated in the exchange market, propelled by underlying economic changes and by waves of speculation. Then the United States devalued the dollar; it left the gold standard in 1933 and came back to gold at a lower parity in 1934. The countries that had stayed with gold, including France and Italy, imposed new trade barriers to protect themselves against the competition of countries that had quit the gold standard and allowed their currencies to depreciate. Some governments went further, seeking to generate export surpluses and increase employment at the expense of their neighbors. The situation was not brought under control until 1936, when France and other gold-bloc countries changed their gold parities and arranged a "stand-still" agreement with Britain and the United States, barring a new round of competitive depreciations. When the exchange rates had finally settled down, they were not much different from what they had been before 1931. Here are the percentage depreciations ($-$) in key currencies, based on 1930 exchange rates with the U.S. dollar:

	1932	1934	1936
United Kingdom	-33	$+ 2$	$+ 1$
India	-32	$+ 2$	$+ 1$
Australia	-41	-12	-13
Canada	-13	$+ 1$	0
Italy	0	$+62$	0
Belgium	0	$+68$	$+21$
France	0	$+68$	$+19$

The Commonwealth countries (India, Australia, and Canada) moved with Great Britain; their currencies depreciated through 1932 (for Britain had left gold in 1931), but strengthened in relation to the dollar by 1934 (for the dollar left gold in 1933). The gold-bloc countries, by contrast, showed no change until 1934, when the drop in the gold price of the dollar raised the dollar price of their currencies. By 1936, however, much of this premium had vanished; the gold-bloc countries had changed their own gold parities.

Summing up the 1920's and 1930's, one observer drew these conclusions:

> The twenty years between the wars have furnished ample evidence concerning the question of fluctuating *versus* stable exchanges. A system of completely free and flexible exchange rates is conceivable and may have certain attractions in theory. . . . Yet nothing would be more at variance with the lessons of the past. . . . In the first place, they create an element of risk which tends to discourage international trade. . . . Secondly, as a means of adjusting

81

the balance of payments, exchange fluctuations involve constant shifts of labour and other resources between production for the home market and production for export. . . . Thirdly, experience has shown that . . . any considerable or continuous movement of the exchange rate is liable to generate anticipations of a further movement in the same direction, thus giving rise to speculative capital transfers of a disequilibrating kind. . . .[1]

This view had an enormous impact on the monetary system that rose from the wreckage of the Second World War.

The Bretton Woods System

This time, the governments avoided one of the grave errors they had committed after the First World War. They tried to deal separately with the needs of postwar reconstruction, rather than burdening the international monetary system with a new layer of indebtedness and straining the new system of exchange rates with abnormal import needs. The U.S. Lend-Lease program gave outright aid to America's allies in order to forestall the accumulation of new intergovernmental debts. A large U.S. loan to Britain in 1945 and the Marshall Plan of 1948 sought to finance reconstruction without drawing off the gold reserves of the war-shattered countries or saddling them with huge short-term obligations.

Governments likewise sought to work out new exchange rates by general agreement and to keep them stable once they had been fixed. They did not foreswear all exchange-rate changes, preferring devaluation to exchange controls, trade controls or deflation. Devaluation was preferred to exchange or trade controls, because it does not distort resource allocation; it increases the foreign demand for domestic goods in addition to limiting the domestic demand for foreign goods. Import controls, by contrast, increase the domestic price of import-competing products, attracting domestic resources away from the more efficient export industries. Devaluation was preferred to deflation because it does not depress employment or halt economic growth. In modern economies with wage and price rigidity, deflation leads to unemployment before it lowers prices. And every major government is pledged to maintain maximum employment and foster rapid growth.

The new exchange-rate system was enshrined in the Bretton Woods Agreement of 1944, which established the International Monetary Fund (IMF) and erected the framework for postwar monetary cooperation. Governments agreed to peg their currencies to gold or the U.S. dollar (which, in turn, is pegged to gold). They agreed to make their currencies convertible—to dismantle their exchange controls—after a transition period. And they agreed on rules to police exchange-rate changes. A government may alter the par value of its currency

[1]Ragnar Nurkse, *International Currency Experience* (Geneva League of Nations, 1944), pp. 210–211.

by as much as 10 per cent without IMF approval, but needs the Fund's approval for any larger change. This approval, moreover, will be forthcoming only when a country faces a "fundamental disequilibrium" in its international accounts.

The Bretton Woods system, sometimes called the system of the *adjustable peg*, seeks to assure maximum exchange-rate stability, yet to facilitate orderly changes when they are needed and to avoid competitive devaluations like those of the 1930's. There have been important exchange-rate changes under the Bretton Woods system. In 1949 Britain devalued the pound from $4.03 to $2.80, and was followed by many other countries in Europe and the Commonwealth. France devalued the franc in 1957. Germany and the Netherlands raised their parities in 1961. And India devalued the rupee in 1966. Exchange-rate changes have been particularly frequent in the less-developed countries—especially those of Latin America—just as they were in the nineteenth century. The less-developed countries have had difficulty maintaining price stability while seeking to promote more rapid growth; they lack the wide range of policy instruments available to countries have had difficulty maintaining price stability while seeking to promote afflicted by wide fluctuations in the prices of their major export products. In consequence, they have encountered serious balance-of-payments problems.

In the past few years, however, the Bretton Woods system has shown signs of coming unstuck. It has been rocked by a series of shocks that began with a crisis of confidence in sterling and spread to the dollar and the franc. The British were forced to devalue the pound from $2.80 to $2.40 in November 1967, after a string of policy measures—including deflation and substantial borrowing from the IMF and central banks—failed to end her deficit or stem successive waves of speculation. After sterling was devalued, the speculators turned their attention to the dollar or, more precisely, to the gold–dollar link that has served for so long as the cornerstone of the Bretton Woods system. In three gold rushes, in November and December 1967 and March 1968, they speculated on a dollar devaluation that would raise the price of gold. The price of gold in the private London market had been stabilized at $35 per ounce by an arrangement under which eight governments jointly bought or sold gold on the private market to keep the price within a specified range. The speculative buying amounted to a raid on official gold stocks, as the governments involved fed gold to the private market to keep the price down. Some $3 billion of gold flowed out of monetary stocks into private hands in the space of a few months. After a series of optimistic statements, the central bankers finally admitted their inability to stabilize the market and returned to an earlier arrangement; the free market price is unregulated, and the monetary authorities deal among themselves at $35 per ounce.

The franc's turn came in November 1968. The French payments position was seriously weakened by the substantial increases in wages and prices that followed the semi-insurrection of May 1968. The speculators also bet on a *revaluation* of the German mark and large sums of money poured into Germany. The

Germans, despite a large payments surplus, refused to revalue, causing most experts to forecast a French devaluation. But General de Gaulle said no, embarking instead on a program of deflation to defend the existing parity. It was not until de Gaulle's departure, that France, on a quiet weekend in August 1969, devalued by 12.5 per cent.

Finally, the vast inflow of funds into Germany throughout 1969 forced the Bonn Government temporarily to free the mark in the foreign exchange market, then to declare a revaluation of 9.3 per cent in October 1969. As this is written, three major countries have weak currencies—the dollar, the franc, and the pound. All three currencies are clearly subject to further speculative attacks.

The German revaluation may relieve some of the pressure on these other currencies—and is an important precedent—but the promise of exchange-rate stability offered by Bretton Woods may not be honored by forthcoming history.

The Case for Greater Flexibility

Many economists have long forecast the crises of the 1960's. In their view, the Bretton Woods regime combines the disadvantages of fully fixed exchange rates with the disadvantage of flexible exchange rates. First, they say, the Bretton Woods system encourages countries to employ undesirable methods of payments adjustment. Because the system treats a change in the exchange rate as the remedy of last resort, such a change becomes conspicuous rather than an everyday occurrence. Hence governments hesitate to alter their exchange rates; they tend to regard devaluation as a confession of failure. Some governments still resort to trade controls, overt or covert, distorting resource allocation. Others keep a tight rein on domestic demand, using restrictive monetary and fiscal policies; they forego economic growth to maintain payments equilibrium. This has been a common criticism of British policy and, at times, of American policy as well. More generally, critics say, the present system imparts a deflationary bias to the whole process of payments adjustment. A country that runs a payments deficit will eventually use up its reserves. But a surplus country can accumulate reserves indefinitely.[2] A deficit country may therefore be obliged to deflate or devalue its currency, whereas a surplus country cannot be compelled to inflate or appreciate. Under flexible exchange rates, by contrast, the market operates with an even hand, raising the price of the surplus country's currency and lowering the price of the deficit country's currency.

[2] A surplus country may have difficulty offsetting the monetary impact of its payments surplus. To sop up the commerical-bank reserves created by a surplus, the central bank must engage in open-market sales of government securities or must raise commercial-bank reserve requirements. But it can run out of government securities. And by increasing reserve requirements, it ties up the assets of the commercial banks, diminishing bank profits. These things were happening in Germany in 1958–1961, when Germany experienced a massive payments surplus, the counterpart of the U.S. deficit, discussed below. They have led some Europeans to argue that the present system is inflationary, not deflationary, and to charge that Europe has had to "import inflation" from deficit countries, notably the United States.

Critics also accuse the present system of fostering perverse capital movements that aggravate the basic payments problems. Speculation can be *destabilizing*. This is because traders and investors can "attack" a weak currency at negligible cost. Suppose that the price of the pound has fallen from $2.40 to $2.38, as far as it can with its present parity, and that Britain's reserves are slipping away as the Bank of England uses them to support the exchange rate. Speculators know that Britain cannot lose reserves forever, and they may begin to gamble on the possibility that Britain will devalue the pound. Some will sell the sterling securities they hold; others will borrow in London rather than abroad, hoping to repay their debts with cheaper pounds. These flows and others will add to the pressure on the price of the pound and force the Bank of England to use up even more reserves. If devaluation were possible before the speculation began, it can become nearly certain once speculation is underway.

If Britain does devalue the pound, the speculators will reap handsome profits. If the pound is not devalued, they can "unwind" their positions with very little loss; they will be able to buy the pounds they need at a slight additional cost. At worst, the pound will rise to its upper limit, $2.42 exacting a 4¢ premium from speculators when they come to rebuild their sterling holdings and pay off their sterling debts. But 4¢ on $2.40 is a mere 1.67 per cent—hardly a high price to pay for the chance of gaining 20 or 30 per cent from a devaluation.

Speculators can also attack a weak currency under a system of flexible exchange rates. But speculation would be much more costly, for the price of the pound could rise without limit, compelling the speculators to "unwind" their positions at a huge premium. Furthermore, some experts say, a system of flexible exchange rates would actually engender *stabilizing* speculation, rather than *destabilizing* speculation. The activities of speculators would strengthen a weak currency rather than weaken it further.

The debate on this point has grown quite complex. But the basic point at issue is very simple. The advocates of flexible exchange rates argue that a drop in the price of any asset will attract more buyers, not more sellers. When a currency weakens in the foreign-exchange market, speculators will come to regard it as a bargain and will start to buy it. Doing so, they will arrest the decline in its price, and may even cause its price to rise. Likewise, as a currency appreciates, speculators will come to believe that it is priced too high and will start to sell it. Doing so, they will arrest or reverse the rise in price. If these propositions are true, speculation will dampen exchange-rate fluctuations, not amplify them.

This analysis of speculation builds on an implicit supposition that there is a trendless "normal" rate to guide the speculators when they make their judgments about future exchange rates. If there were no "normal" rate (or if it had a trend), speculators could not be so certain that a falling rate would soon start to rise again, or that a rising rate would soon start to fall. They might consequently buy as rates began to rise or sell as rates began to fall, and might then aggravate price fluctuations. The importance of a "normal" rate showed up

85

clearly in the 1950's, when the Canadian dollar was allowed to fluctuate: the exchange rate stayed within a rather narrow range, helped by speculation. But the speculators may have been guided by a fixed norm—the old one-for-one parity between the two currencies. The behavior of the spot and forward rates supports this hypothesis. When the Canadian dollar exceeded its old parity with the U.S. dollar, it dropped to a discount on the forward market; speculators apparently thought the spot rate was "too high," basing their opinions on the old parity.[3]

This need for a "normal" rate implies that exchange-rate flexibility may work most efficiently when the underlying balance-of-payments disturbances do not call for large variations in the rate. If large changes are required and the rate drifts away from its familiar range, speculators may not know which way to turn and may begin to operate in a destabilizing manner.

There is one more objection to full flexibility: it could build an upward bias into world prices. Depreciations and devaluations raise the domestic prices of imported goods; this is how they work to discourage imports. In countries that import foodstuffs or industrial materials, however, an increase in import prices raises the cost of living and evokes a demand for higher wages. Higher wages, in turn, raise prices—including export prices. In brief, an exchange-rate change can touch off a wage-price spiral, offsetting much of the competitive advantage conferred by the initial depreciation or devaluation. If, of course, the increase in wage rates is quite small compared to the depreciation, the depreciation will still serve to eliminate a payment deficit, and a country facing a deep-seated payments problem should accept depreciation. But what of a country whose foreign transactions display a cyclical pattern, showing a deficit during a boom and a surplus during a recession? If its exchange rate fluctuated freely, its currency would depreciate during a boom, adding to domestic inflationary pressures. It would, of course, appreciate during the next recession, but its wage rates might not come back down. With flexible exchange rates, then, the domestic business cycle would raise wages and prices in a stepwise fashion.

One could adduce another dozen arguments on each side of this issue—and as many intermediate positions. Some economists, for example, argue that fixed parities are needed, if only to provide speculators with the necessary "norm," but advocate wider margins for fluctuations on each side of parity. These wider margins, they contend, would raise the cost of speculating against a weak currency. If the pound could fall as low as $2.30 and rise as high as $2.50, speculators could lose 20¢ on the pound over a single swing, and 20¢ on $2.40 is an 8 per cent loss, much larger than the present 1.67 per cent. Further, with wider margins, the exchange rates could fluctuate sufficiently (by, say, 5 per cent on either side of parity) to have strong price effects on imports and exports.

[3]Paul Wonnacott, *The Canadian Dollar, 1948–1962* (Toronto: University of Toronto Press, 1965), p. 188.

Another scheme proposes a fixed parity that would change by small discrete steps (by a maximum, say, of 2 percentage points a year). This proposal would allow a government to adjust its parity without the destabilizing speculation that has usually accompanied or forced large parity changes. Still other proposals seek to combine this "crawling peg" with wider margins. Under such a scheme, the exchange-rate parity might be adjusted whenever the rate was at its floor or ceiling for a stated period of time.

These intermediate proposals have been advanced by academic economists, attempting to sell governments and central banks on an acceptable version of a flexible-rate system. Official thinking has not yet accepted the need for greater flexibility though governments have shown greater interest in the very recent past. Despite the apparent need for greater flexibility, reforms that stand a chance of adoption seem likely to be limited, as officials still prefer to use their reserves in support of existing exchange rates, even to adjust domestic policies to correct imbalances, rather than change exchange rates frequently or automatically.

The New Gold-Exchange Standard

The central banks would seem to have sufficient reserves both for combating speculation in the foreign-exchange markets and for buying time in which to make gradual adjustments. At the end of 1969, central banks and governments held some $77 billion of gold and foreign currencies (Table 5–1), a sum more than one-third the dollar value of world exports, and many times larger than the largest annual reserve flow (the sum of all deficits) in recent years. Most of these reserves, moreover, were held at the center of the interna-

Table 5–1   INTERNATIONAL MONETARY RESERVES, 1958 AND 1969

(billions of dollars; end of year)

Country or Area	1958	1969
United States	22.5	16.9
United Kingdom	3.1	2.5
Total, reserve centers	25.6	19.4
European Economic Community*	12.2	20.9
Canada and Japan	3.1	6.8
Other developed countries**	5.4	10.4
Total, all developed countries	46.3	57.5
Other European countries	1.8	4.6
Latin America	3.3	4.5
Other Asian and African countries	6.0	10.5
Total, less-developed countries	11.0	19.6
Total, all countries	57.5	76.9

*Belgium–Luxembourg, France, Germany, Italy, and the Netherlands.
**Austria, Denmark, Norway, Sweden, Switzerland, Australia, New Zealand, and South Africa.
Source: International Monetary Fund, *International Financial Statistics* (various issues).

tional monetary system. A full $40 billion belonged to eight governments—the United States, the United Kingdom, and six countries of the European Common Market. Furthermore, the center countries have substantial drawing rights on the International Monetary Fund,[4] and have established an impressive network of bilateral credit arrangements, giving them access to each other's currencies when they need to supplement their national reserves. Until recently, most authorities were satisfied with the level of world reserves, though many were worried about their distribution, composition, and future expansion.

During the past decade or so, continental Europe has increased its reserves at a very rapid rate; indeed the EEC by itself added $19 billion to its holdings between 1958 and 1969. But Britain has stood still for more than a decade, and does not have enough reserves, given the importance of sterling as an international currency. Furthermore, the less-developed countries have gained very little, and lack the cash assets required to deal with their payments problems. It is sometimes said that the low-income countries would *spend* any increase in reserves because they need foreign exchange for development—that any redistribution of reserves would not last long because the low-income countries would soon run down their holdings to their original low levels. This is probably true, but does not dispel concern that those levels are too low and that, in consequence, the less-developed countries are forced into premature policy measures, including resort to import restrictions, whenever they lapse into deficit.

Table 5–2 THE COMPOSITION OF INTERNATIONAL MONETARY RESERVES 1958 AND 1969 (billions of dollars; end of year)

Country and Asset	1958	1969
United States	22.5	16.9
Gold	20.6	11.9
Foreign exchange*	1.9	5.0
All other countries	34.9	60.0
Gold	17.4	27.3
Foreign exchange*	17.5	32.7
U.S. dollars	9.6	16.2
Sterling	7.0	8.9
IMF *gold-tranche* positions	0.6	4.4
Other**	0.3	3.2
Total Reserves	59.5	76.9

*Includes *gold-tranche* drawing rights on the International Monetary Fund.
**Derived as a residual (the difference between total foreign-exchange assets reported by the holders and the foreign-exchange liabilities reported by the United States and United Kingdom). The 1969 figure may include some dollars held outside the United States and some official holdings of long-term securities.
Source: International Monetary Fund, *International Financial Statistics* (various issues).

[4] So-called *gold-tranche* drawing rights are included in reserves, as shown in Table 5–2, for they correspond to the gold subscriptions governments made to obtain their quotas in the IMF, and may be drawn automatically when countries are in deficit. Drawing rights beyond the *gold tranche* are not included in reserves because they are not automatic.

Some economists, in short, are worried that the global level of reserves, substantial as it seems, has not grown rapidly enough compared to the growth of world trade. Reserves as a proportion of world imports fell from 50 per cent in 1960 to 34 per cent in 1968. Moreover, the *sources* of recent reserve growth raise acute concern about the composition of reserves. Outside the United States, reserves are evenly divided between gold and currencies (see Table 5–2). The U.S. dollar is the leading reserve currency, accounting for more than a quarter of other countries' reserve assets. But the United States has actually supplied more than three fifths of the increase in other countries' reserves since 1958. It has furnished $6.6 billion of dollar assets and $8.7 billion of gold (the other $1.0 billion of gold coming from new production and Soviet sales).[5] The $8.7 billion gold loss and $6.6 billion increase in U.S. debts are the consequence of deficits in the United States balance of payments.

The United States is far from insolvency, despite this deterioration in its own reserve position. Table 5–3 shows that the total foreign assets of the United States greatly exceed its total liabilities, and that the excess of assets over liabilities has grown tremendously since 1950. But many observers are not impressed with this calculation; they look, instead, at the U.S. cash position, and this has weakened markedly. There has been an $8.6 billion decline in the official mone-

Table 5–3 THE INTERNATIONAL INVESTMENT POSITION OF THE UNITED STATES, 1950 AND 1968 (billions of dollars; end of year)

Item	1950	1968
Total Assets	54.4	146.1
Official monetary assets (gold and foreign exchange)	24.3	15.7
Private monetary assets (claims on foreigners)	1.5	13.0
Private direct investments abroad	11.8	64.8
Other private long-term investments abroad	5.7	24.2
Other government claims on foreigners	11.1	28.5
Total Liabilities	17.6	81.1
Monetary liabilities to foreign governments*	3.7	17.5
Monetary liabilities to other foreigners	5.9	19.4
Foreign private direct investments	3.4	10.8
Other foreign long-term investments	4.6	33.4
Excess of Assets over Liabilities		
All assets less all liabilities	36.8	65.0
Official monetary assets less official monetary liabilities	20.6	− 1.8

*Figure for 1968 includes certain U.S. obligations that do not appear in the corresponding 1969 total of dollar reserves given in Table 5–2.
Source: United States Department of Commerce, *Survey of Current Business* (October, 1969).

[5] Another cause for concern is that total stock of gold in *official* hands (countries plus international agencies) has fallen since 1965, as industrial demand and speculative buying have outstripped new production (Soviet sales have virtually ceased since 1965).

tary assets of the United States and a $13.8 billion increase in its liabilities to foreign governments and central banks, making for a $22.4 billion decline in the net cash figure.[6]

The gold-buying of late 1967 and March 1968 dramatized the vulnerability of the U.S. dollar. A continuing balance-of-payments deficit, worsened by the Vietnam war, eroded international confidence in the U.S. dollar to such a degree that a sterling devaluation was expected to trigger a massive attack on the dollar. Even now, however, the dollar has many defenses. The United States still holds a third of the world's gold, and though the dollar holdings of foreign governments are larger than U.S. reserves, those dollars are widely held, and most of them are firmly lodged. No single government could carry off a large part of the U.S. gold stock, and few would be inclined to try. Most governments and central banks recognize that a major run on the dollar is an attack upon the stability of the international monetary system itself, and that such an attack would damage the entire global network of trade and payments. This recognition engendered official support for the dollar in 1968 and the determination to maintain its central position in the international monetary system.

But what about the long-term future? Some economists have warned that the present connection between the U.S. balance of payments and the U.S. balance sheet as a supplier of reserves may be unhealthy for the United States and for the international monetary system. The assets and liabilities of an ordinary commercial bank move in the same direction. When its customers draw down their deposits, the bank's cash holdings and liabilities fall together. But the cash assets and liabilities of the United States, acting as an international bank, may move in opposite directions because its balance is linked with its transactions as a producer, consumer, and investor—with its balance of payments. When the United States slips into deficit, it loses gold and, simultaneously, incurs additional deposit obligations to foreign governments. Its cash position tends to deteriorate at the very time when the outside world comes into possession of additional dollars. If, then the United States runs a large or long deficit in its international transactions, its depositors may not want to hold more dollars—or those they already possess—and may then compound the payments problems of the United States by cashing in their dollars. Concerned with these difficulties, governments and academic economists have sought to alter the connection between the United States' balance of payments and the international monetary system—to forestall any sudden switch from dollars to gold and to furnish an increase in total reserves when such an increase is needed.

These two tasks are closely connected. To forestall a shift from dollars

---

[6]Some people are also concerned about the $13.5 billion increase in U.S. short-term obligations to other foreigners, and do not take much comfort from the $11.5 billion increase in U.S. private short-term claims, for those include bank loans and commercial credits, which the government could not easily mobilize in order to defend the dollar.

to gold, the United States must eliminate its payments deficit, for this would bolster confidence in the dollar as a reserve currency. But when it has done so, the growth of total reserves could come to a halt. United States deficits have been the chief source of reserves for other countries, and new gold production has ceased to furnish additional reserves to meet future needs. It has been suggested that governments might increase the price of gold, as this would raise the dollar value of existing gold stocks and stimulate new gold production. But an increase in the price of gold might aggravate the problem of stability by damaging confidence in the dollar.

The New Role of the International Monetary Fund

Many of these worries over liquidity and stability may soon be resolved by the decision to create a new reserve asset—Special Drawing Rights in the International Monetary Fund. This decision, ratified in 1969, was the end-product of the IMF's postwar experience and of numerous reform proposals coming from scholars and governments alike. We will first look at the Fund and its evolution, before turning to the reform adopted in 1969.[7]

The IMF General Account does not create reserves in significant amounts. It merely makes them "go around" more efficiently. It is a pool of currencies and gold furnished by its 103 member governments. When a country joins the IMF, it is assigned a *quota* that governs the size of its cash subscription, its voting power, and its drawing rights. The United States has the largest quota ($5,160 million), Lebanon the smallest ($6.75 million). A member country pays a quarter of its quota in gold and the balance in its own currency. Thus, the United States has paid in $1,290 million of gold and $3,870 million of special U.S. government securities.

When a country encounters a payments deficit and does not have sufficient reserves to cope with the problem, it can buy foreign currencies from the IMF in exchange for its own currency, but it must repurchase its own currency within five years. A member of the IMF is always entitled to buy foreign currencies equal in value to a quarter of its quota (the equivalent of its initial gold subscription, or *gold tranche*). To make a larger purchase, it must satisfy the Fund that it is trying to solve its payments problem, as by controlling domestic inflation. Thus, the Fund is able to exert a unique influence on national policies. In the words of a former Fund official:

> . . . when a country is clearly in such an unbalanced position that radical measures are required to restore equilibrium, private banks may properly be deterred by the risks involved in granting it further credit facilities. In such situations, it is only if a comprehensive program is adopted and put into effect that the risks will be reduced; and private institutions are not in a position to

[7]The Special Drawing Rights facility forms a Special Account in the IMF. The pre-1970 structure is now denoted the General Account. When we speak simply of the IMF we mean this General Account.

negotiate such programs. Experience has shown that the Governments in the various countries are more willing to discuss and work out stabilization programs with officials of the Fund than with representatives of other countries or of private credit institutions.

The IMF has proved its usefulness. In 22 years, it has supplied 23 different currencies to 66 countries, in amounts totaling $18 billion. Britain has been the largest single beneficiary of IMF assistance, as Britain's own reserves are very small and the foreign-exchange markets have forecast devaluation whenever Britain has run into deficit. The less-developed countries have also made extensive use of IMF resources. They, too, have small reserves and chronic payments problems. Their imports have risen rapidly because of their efforts to stimulate development. And many of them earn their way in world trade by exporting raw materials—coffee, tin, and copper—that are subject to unusually wide price fluctuations.

The IMF has expanded several times during its history. There were substantial revisions of quotas in 1959 and 1965, and another increase was approved in 1969, to go into effect in 1971. This continuous growth in quotas has served partially to substitute for a straightforward increase in national reserves. Admittedly, governments have to put more gold into the IMF to obtain larger quotas. But they obtain a $4 increase in quotas (and an even larger increase in drawing rights) for every dollar's worth of gold paid in. The IMF has also helped negotiate special defensive arrangements for the key currencies and to forestall major shifts in reserve composition.

Unfortunately, the IMF's *usable* assets are much smaller than its total assets ($21 billion). At the end of 1969, IMF holdings of gold and major currencies looked like this:

Gold	$ 2.3 billion
United States dollars	2.8 "
Sterling	4.7 "
EEC currencies	3.1 "
Other key currencies	1.1 "
Total	$14.0 "

The Fund, moreover, cannot use all those assets at the same time. If the U.S. dollar were in trouble, the Fund could not use dollars to help out; it would have to use gold and other convertible currencies, and might not have enough to combat speculation against a key currency.[8] Hence many proponents of reform, while welcoming a stronger IMF, were nevertheless worried. They wanted to sever all connections between the U.S. balance of payments and the creation of reserves,

[8]In 1962, ten key countries, including the United States, did agree on procedures for lending to the IMF should it need additional currencies to finance a major drawing. These are known as the Group of Ten: the United States, France, Germany, the United Kingdom, Italy, Belgium, the Netherlands, Canada, Japan, and Sweden. Their agreement is called the General Arrangements to Borrow.

because American deficits could still undermine the monetary system and because the United States cannot change its own exchange rate without breaking the link between gold and the dollar. Finally, the critics said, an increase in IMF quotas may not be a satisfactory substitute for larger reserves because drawings on the Fund must be repaid.

The leading advocate of reform was Professor Robert Triffin of Yale. He suggested that the International Monetary Fund be transformed into a central bankers' bank—that central banks deposit a percentage of their gross reserves with the IMF, and that these deposits be denominated in a new international unit of account.[9]

This arrangement, Triffin argued, would have two advantages. First, deposits at the IMF would carry a gold guarantee. If there were an increase in the dollar price of gold (a devaluation of the dollar), the value of an IMF deposit would not be affected, whereas a dollar deposit would buy less gold thereafter. Governments would have little cause to change the composition of their reserves. Second, the IMF could enlarge total reserves in much the same way that a national central bank enlarges the reserves of the commercial banks. It could create a new type of money. Instead of selling foreign currency to a country needing more reserves, the Fund would make straightforward loans, creating new deposits to the credit of the borrower. The borrower could then draw on its deposit to settle deficits with other governments—or could use its balance to buy foreign currencies for use in the foreign-exchange markets. Finally, the IMF would be authorized to buy national securities in the open market, much in the manner of a central bank conducting open-market operations, so as to create more IMF money and thereby enlarge world reserves.

Triffin's plan would have limited lending by the IMF, to prevent an excessive expansion of world reserves. Lending could not exceed what would be required to augment reserves by 3 or 4 per cent a year. His plan also allowed any central bank to convert its "excess" IMF deposits into gold or currency—to dispose of deposits it was not obliged to hold under the prevailing reserve ratio. Thus, no country would have to accept indefinite amounts of IMF deposit money.

Other plans were then devised to repair apparent defects in Triffin's proposal. Still others would have linked the creation of new reserves to the international financing of economic development. Under these plans, the IMF would buy bonds from intergovernmental agencies like the International Bank for Reconstruction and Development, supplying these agencies with IMF deposits that could then be lent to the less-developed countries.

Most of these plans met with frowns from governments and central banks. There was an understandable resistance to radical reform. The governments,

[9]Triffin suggested that they be required to deposit 20 per cent of their reserves, but believes that most governments would voluntarily keep a larger fraction on deposit with the IMF, as these deposits would earn interest and be guaranteed against exchange-rate changes. Triffin's plan, incidentally, had distinguished antecedents, including a proposal by Lord Keynes, offered as an alternative to the United States' plan for the IMF when the Fund was set up in 1944.

however, came gradually to favor reform and in 1967, after three years of tortuous negotiations, agreed upon a plan. Their plan was approved by the IMF in September 1967, achieved the required number of ratifications by 1969, and came into effect in 1970.

The new plan establishes a separate facility at the IMF, known as the Special Drawing Account, containing Special Drawings Rights (SDRs). All members of the IMF will receive allocations of SDRs in proportion to their current IMF quotas. SDRs can be used by a deficit country to acquire foreign currencies from another country. The nation providing the currency (its own or a third country's) receives an equivalent amount of SDRs on the IMF's books. Each government has the clear right to use its SDRs, and a country offered SDRs in exchange for currency is obliged to accept them (and can, of course, use them should it need them in the future). There are just two limitations on the use of SDRs. A country cannot use all its SDRs all of the time; it must maintain a 30 per cent average minimum balance over the first five-year period of issue. Further, no country is obliged to accept SDRs if its holdings already exceed 300 per cent of its cumulative allocation. The first limitation leaves the SDR somewhere between money and credit; a country must repurchase SDRs if its holdings fall below the 30 per cent limit for any length of time. Under the second limitation, moreover, a surplus country need not accept unlimited amounts of SDRs.

The size of the initial SDR allocation was a matter of prolonged contention. The United States pressed for a much larger-size issue than the Europeans wanted. The parties finally agreed on $3.5 billion for the first year (1970), and $3.0 billion for the next two years. To illustrate the large potential liquidity creation involved, suppose $3.0 billion of SDRs a year are issued for 15 years. At the end of 15 years, $45 billion of SDRs would exist, an amount larger than the present gold holdings of all central banks. With a $3.5 billion initial allocation, moreover, the United States is due to receive $867 million; Great Britain, $410 million; France, $165 million; and Germany, $202 million.

Most economists consider the SDRs a major improvement in the international monetary system. A solution of the U.S. balance-of-payments problem no longer threatens to dry up the major source of increased international liquidity. The larger volume of liquidity, moreover, will give governments more time for adjustment, lessening their need to use undesirable adjustment policies. SDRs, however, will not cure all that now ails us.

First, it is not clear that recent international financial instability was caused by inadequate liquidity. A speculative attack on a currency can succeed even in the face of large reserves, or can eat up enough reserves to lay a country open to a future successful attack. Ten years of SDR creation would give France no more than $2 billion of extra reserves. France had nearly $7 billion of reserves at the beginning of 1968, but was forced to devalue within less than two years. Second, the adjustment problem under fixed exchange rates is not yet resolved. Liquidity can buy time, but satisfactory adjustment mechanisms are not available to use that time effectively. Many of the problems of the Bretton Woods regime are still with us.

THE UNITED STATES PAYMENTS PROBLEM

Future international financial stability requires an end to the large deficit in the balance of payments. No amount of financing, no special arrangements, can sustain international confidence in the dollar if U.S. gold holdings begin again to shrink and liabilities continue to grow. Elimination of the U.S. deficit must be a major policy target.

The United States has run payments deficits since the early 1950's. In the late 1950's, however, its deficits grew very large, averaging more than $2 billion yearly from 1958 through 1964 and $1.5 billion from 1965 to 1967. The deficit seemed to have been eliminated in 1968 and 1969 as we shall see, but this improvement was more illusory than real.

Part of the large deficit can be blamed on the inflation of the 1950's. Table 5–4 shows that U. S. export prices rose rather rapidly from 1955 through 1960.

Table 5–4 PERCENTAGE INCREASE IN EXPORT PRICES, MAJOR INDUSTRIAL COUNTRIES, 1955–1960, 1960–1964, AND 1964–1968

Country	1955–1960	1960–1964	1964–1968
United States	+7	+ 2	+10
Belgium	0	0	+ 1
Canada	+6	− 5	+13
France	−1	+ 6	+ 2
Germany	+5	+ 7	0
Italy	−8	+ 1	− 6
Japan	−4	− 5	+ 1
Netherlands	0	+ 7	0
Sweden	0	+ 2	+ 1
Switzerland	0	+14	+14
United Kingdom	+9	+ 6	− 1

Source: International Monetary Fund, International Financial Statistics (various issues).

The over-all (consumer) price index did not behave poorly, compared to the price indexes of other countries, but a sharp advance in steel prices raised many export prices. The United States did not lose too much ground in world markets, but neither did it gain sufficiently to cover its growing import bill, its military spending, or the surge in private foreign investment.

In the early 1960's, U.S. prices rose somewhat less rapidly than those of other countries, and the U.S. trade balance improved dramatically; from 1960 through 1964, average annual merchandise exports were $5.3 billion larger than merchandise imports (see Table 5–5). Furthermore, earnings on American investments abroad were $3.3 billion larger than foreign earnings from the United States. Yet the payments deficit did not subside, for there was a further increase in military spending, foreign aid, and private investment. In the five-year period 1960–1964, net outlays on foreign aid (grants and loans) and military spending averaged $5.5 billion, and U.S. private investment accounted for $4.6 billion more per annum.

The picture from 1965 on is complex (emphasizing that we must look behind a single statistic to the underlying, detailed components). The balance on official settlements, defined in Chapter 4, indicated a *surplus* for 1966, 1968, and 1969. The underlying situation, however, was extremely serious. Though foreign aid and private investments leveled out—the latter because of selective policy aimed directly at them—they remained at high levels. At the same time, military spending rose because of the Vietnam War. But the most ominous development, connected to rapid domestic expansion, was the swing toward deficit on trade account:

	1964	1968
Exports	25.3	33.6
Imports	18.6	33.0
Trade balance	6.7	0.6

Exports grew handsomely, but imports came near to doubling in four years! Inflation explains a large part of the problem. Table 5–4 shows the sharp rise in U.S. export prices since 1964.

This sharp deterioration in the trade balance has been offset by huge foreign investments in the United States; in 1968, they grew by $10 billion ($6.5 billion on capital account and $3.5 billion on cash account) and in 1969 by $13.6 billion ($4.4 on capital account and $9.2 billion on cash account). But these cannot be expected to continue for long. Large borrowings abroad by U.S. corporations are due to our own direct-investment controls, and there have been large European purchases on U.S. stock markets. The cash account, moreover, has been hugely distorted by large short-term foreign borrowings on the part of U.S. banks, responding to extremely tight credit conditions in the United States. Thus, the enduring payments deficit has been masked by volatile capital inflows. The trade balance, on the other hand, may continue to worsen if U.S. prices continue to rise.

The United States has taken many measures to reduce its deficit. In the 1950's, it "tied" most of its foreign aid to the purchase of American goods and services and cut down on overseas spending by its armed forces, compelling the Defense Department to "buy American" whenever possible. In effect, it imposed a covert tariff on government spending abroad, forcing government agencies (and the taxpayer) to spend more for goods and services. Then, in 1963, the United States imposed a tax on purchases of foreign securities (except

Table 5–5   THE U.S. BALANCE OF PAYMENTS, 1960–1964, 1965–1968 AND 1969 (billions of dollars)

Item	1960–1964 Average	1965–1968 Average	1969
Exports of goods and services	31.1	44.8	55.4
Merchandise exports	21.5	30.0	36.5
Transport, travel, and other services	4.6	7.0	8.5
Military receipts	0.6	1.1	1.5
Income on U.S. investments abroad	4.4	6.6	8.9
Imports of goods and services	−25.2	−39.8	−53.3
Merchandise imports	−16.2	−26.7	−35.8
Transport, travel, and other services	− 4.9	− 6.9	− 8.2
Military expenditures	− 3.0	− 3.9	− 4.9
Income on foreign investments in U.S.	− 1.1	− 2.3	− 4.4
Unilateral transfers (net)	− 2.6	− 2.9	− 2.8
Government grants	− 1.8	− 1.8	− 1.7
Other transfers	− 0.8	− 1.1	− 1.1
Balance on current account	3.3	2.1	− 0.7
Capital account [net outflow (−)]	− 4.4	− 4.0	− 1.9
U.S. government credits and claims	− 1.3	− 1.9	− 2.2
U.S. private direct investment abroad	− 1.9	− 3.4	− 3.1
Other U.S. private lending and investment abroad	− 1.7	− 1.2	− 1.0
Foreign investment and lending in U.S.	0.5	2.5	4.4
Errors and omissions	− 0.9	− 0.7	− 3.0
Balance on current and capital accounts	− 2.0	− 2.6	− 5.6
Cash account			
Private holdings and claims	− 0.2	1.9	8.3
U.S. claims on foreigners [increase (−)]	− 1.0	− 0.1	− 0.9
Foreign claims on U.S. [increase (+)]	0.8	2.0	9.2
Official holdings and claims (net deficit)	− 2.2	− 0.7	2.7
U.S. reserve assets [increase (−)]	1.0	0.2	− 1.2
Foreign official dollar holdings [increase (+)]	1.2	0.5	− 1.5

Source: United States Department of Commerce, Survey of Current Business (various issues). Private holdings and claims in the cash account are those reported by U.S. banks; all other short-term credits and claims appear in the capital account. Foreign official dollar holdings are those used to compute the official settlements measure of the deficit; all other official claims appear as foreign investment in the U.S.

those of Canada and the less-developed countries), and in 1965, applied this same tax to long-term foreign loans by U.S. banks. It also asked U.S. banks to hold down their foreign loans, and made a similar appeal to companies with foreign branches or affiliates, asking that they postpone or pare down new capital commitments and that they borrow abroad for projects that could not be postponed. Finally, in 1968, the government introduced mandatory controls on direct investment, placing a total embargo on new capital outflows to continental Europe and a ceiling on the fraction of total earnings that could be retained abroad for reinvestment. Severe limits were also placed on investment elsewhere.

What more can be done to end the payments problem? Some people have urged that the United States make further cuts in foreign aid, but if aid is cut, exports will fall too, eroding the current account. Of the $5.3 billion in new grants and loans in 1968, fully $4.7 billion were spent in the United States. A cut in military expenditures abroad would be a clear gain for the balance of payments; these expenditures, however, are governed by political, not balance of payments, considerations. Proposals to limit American tourist spending were made by the administration in 1968 and died a quick, merciful death in Congress.

Any other country confronting a similar problem could resort to devaluation —which would enlarge its exports, reduce its imports, and make room for capital or government transactions—but the United States is not free to do so. A devaluation of the dollar would undoubtedly improve our balance of payments, but it would rupture the link between gold and the dollar, damaging the whole monetary system. In addition, a devaluation of the dollar is apt to provoke retaliation; because it would improve the competitive position of the world's largest country, it would damage the foreign trade of other countries, including some countries that do not have surpluses. Those countries, including Canada, Japan, and the United Kingdom, might be forced to devalue after us, and the process might well spread, as in the 1930's, for its impact would come to be concentrated on a smaller and smaller cluster of countries that had not yet changed their exchange rates. In the end, there might be little change in the system of exchange rates, and the United States would reap little benefit.

The United States has battled with its balance of payments for ten years, yet the problem seems as intractable as ever. Price stability is a prerequisite to restore a current-account surplus large enough to cover capital and government transactions. But, as this is written, price stability seems far away—and cannot be brought nearer without paying an intolerable social cost in unemployment.

SUMMARY

Long before the end of the Second World War, governments began to plan the reconstruction of the international monetary system. Determined to avoid another round of competitive exchange-rate changes like the one that followed the First World War, they decided to establish new exchange rates at the very start of the postwar period and to foster orderly changes thereafter. In the Bretton Woods agreement of 1944 establishing the International Monetary Fund, they agreed to forego devaluations, save on occasions of "fundamental disequilibrium."

One can make a strong case against the present system. By pegging exchange rates, it fixes the one set of prices that could be changed with sufficient ease and speed to maintain payments equilibrium. And by compromising between a perfect fixity and full flexibility, it invites destabilizing capital movements that add to payments deficits. Finally, one can argue that a free market would choose the "right" exchange rate more accurately than a finance minister or central banker.

Yet there are telling objections to full flexibility, and some of the defects of the present system could be removed if the gold-exchange standard were strengthened or reformed—if exchange rates could vary more widely around their fixed parities, or could adjust gradually to the payments situation, and if the supply of reserves could be disconnected from the American balance of payments.

The decision to create SDRs divorces liquidity creation from the U.S. payments deficit. But little improvement has been made in the adjustment mechanism.

Finally, you have glanced at the U.S. payments problem and examined the constraints on American policy that make it so difficult for the United States to end its payments deficit. All of the issues and policy conflicts described in Chapter 4 find ample expression in the American experience—and all of the temptations to restrict foreign trade and payments are manifest in recent American policy.

Toward

an International Economy

CHAPTER SIX

THE CENTER AND PERIPHERY

A country's economic history has a tremendous effect on its comparative advantage; indeed, its stocks of capital and skill may influence its foreign trade more than its store of raw materials, climate, or terrain do. These stocks are the legacies of economic history—of investments made in years gone by. And these investments, in their turn, reflect still earlier trade patterns and market opportunities. The evolution of the international economy has been a cumulative process. Export opportunities, affecting the volume and pattern of investment, have shaped each country's stock of capital equipment. Those stocks of equipment, with the skills that accompany them, gave rise to new production possibilities, creating new trade patterns.

Foreign trade has been especially significant for the economic development of new countries, including the United States. Their resource endowments—their stocks of capital and skill—were shaped by their contact with the older countries of the international economy. As John Henry Williams of Harvard has put it:

> The development of international trade has been a process in which the countries outside the centre have owed the development of their trade, and indeed their very existence, to the movement, not merely of goods but of capital, labour, and entrepreneurship from the centre; and the centre countries have in turn owed their further development primarily to this movement. Western Europe created the modern world and was in turn remade by it. Any theory of international trade that does not approach the subject-matter in this way must have very serious limitations as a guide to policy.[1]

[1] John H. Williams, *Trade, Not Aid: A Program for World Stability*. The Stamp Memorial Lecture, 1952 (Cambridge: Harvard University Press, 1953), p. 10.

And the late Ragnar Nurkse of Columbia dwelt on this same theme:

> The industrial revolution happened to originate on a small island with a limited range of natural resources, at a time when synthetic materials were yet unknown. In these circumstances economic expansion was transmitted to less-developed areas by a steep and steady increase in Britain's demand for primary commodities which those areas were well suited to produce. Local factors of production overseas, whose growth may in part have been induced by trade, were thus largely absorbed by the expansion of profitable primary production for export. On top of this, the center's increasing demand for raw materials and foodstuffs created incentives for capital and labor to move from the center to the outlying areas, accelerating the process of growth-transmission from the former to the latter.[2]

Some economists hold to the hope that trade can still serve as an "engine of growth" to quicken the development of Africa, Asia, and Latin America, and that private capital will venture out from the center of the world economy—from the United States and Europe—to find new raw materials and create new industries. They argue that the case for comparative advantage applies with particular force to the less-developed countries, as it is essential for a poor country, through international specialization, to squeeze the maximum possible use out of its limited resources.

It is bad advice, these economists say, to tell a poor country to waste precious resources producing at home goods that can be obtained more cheaply abroad. These defenders of classical theory reject the suggestion that the doctrine of comparative advantage is static—indicating how to get the most out of a given factor endowment—and is of little use to a country that, pursuing economic development, must expand its resources. International specialization, they reply, enables a country to achieve higher levels of real income and, therefore, higher rates of saving and capital accumulation. International trade also enables producers to reap economies of scale, where they exist, by enlarging the market. In brief, these economists assert that poor countries, like others before them, can develop by exporting traditional primary products to import consumer goods and capital goods for industrialization.

Other economists, however, challenge these arguments. Developing countries, they say, have several legitimate grounds for interfering with free trade. We have already met the infant-industry argument, which can sometimes justify temporary tariffs to foster industrialization.

We have also pointed out that the private entrepreneur, following market signals will ignore the *nonmarket* benefits and costs of his decisions. These non-market effects, called *external economies* and *diseconomies*, are alleged to be particularly important in poor countries. For example, an entrepreneur will ignore *linkages* between different stages of production, which must be included in any

[2]Ragnar Nurkse, "Patterns of Trade and Development," reprinted in *Equilibrium and Growth in the World Economy* (Cambridge: Harvard University Press, 1961), p. 285.

full economic valuation of an investment. A decision to place a tariff on a consumer good import in order to encourage domestic producers to perform final assembly may be justified if an increase in assembly stimulates the efficient domestic production of some of the parts.

Another argument for protection points to market imperfections, alleged to be endemic in low-income countries, that distort factor prices, so that these prices will not reflect the true social cost of employing various factors. An entrepreneur responding to distorted market prices will make economically inefficient decisions. It is said, for example, that market wage rates in the manufacturing sector in poor countries are apt to overstate the true social cost of labor, and will cause under-investment in manufacturing. Government intervention to offset these distortions frequently involves the use of tariffs, because they are easy to administer, although other kinds of intervention, such as subsidies, might be economically more efficient. It is hard to know how often the conditions used to justify intervention really exist, and all of these arguments are clearly subject to abuse.

Critics of the classical position also state that nineteenth-century experience is a poor guide to our international economy. They point out that the new countries of the nineteenth century were quite different from today's less-developed countries. The United States, Canada, and Australia lay in temperate zones and had vast quantities of land with very little labor. They could supply the grain and cotton Europe required. Furthermore, they were peopled by immigrants with European institutions and values. Most of today's less-developed countries, by contrast, lie in the tropics, are densely populated, and are not mere islands of European civilization, but have institutions and values of their own.

Furthermore, trade patterns have changed since the nineteenth century. The center countries' need for raw materials is not growing the way it did in the nineteenth century. Production at the center tends to be resource-saving rather than resource-using; the raw materials content of national output is a smaller fraction of the whole than a century ago; value added by processing is very much larger. The development of synthetic materials has also reduced the demand for some raw materials, notably cotton and wool.

Finally, the less-developed countries do not welcome private foreign capital because it has colonial overtones. Nor are they willing forever to remain suppliers of raw materials. They fear the instability of raw-materials prices and foresee a downward trend. They are inclined to draw back from dependence on world markets. Above all, they identify development with industrialization, and seek to build modern industrial facilities to symbolize their independence and assert their maturity. How closely they follow the ancient advice of Alexander Hamilton's *Report on Manufactures:*

> The foreign demand for the products of agricultural countries, is in a great degree, rather casual and occasional, than certain or constant . . . there are natural causes tending to render the external demand for the surplus of agricultural nations a precarious reliance. . . .

Considering how fast and how much the progress of new settlements in the United States must increase the surplus produce of the soil . . . there appear strong reasons to regard the foreign demand for that surplus as too uncertain a reliance, and to desire a substitute for it, in an extensive domestic market.

To secure such a market, there is no other expedient, than to promote manufacturing establishments.

Table 6–1   TRADE BETWEEN DEVELOPED AND LESS-DEVELOPED COUNTRIES IN 1967

Trade Flow	Value in Billions of Dollars	Percentage of World Trade	Percentage Increase Since 1957
1. World exports	178.7	100	85
2. Exports of developed countries	141.3	79	93
a. To developed countries	111.4	62	117
b. To less-developed countries	29.9	17	37
3. Exports of less-developed countries	37.4	21	52
a. To developed countries	29.0	16	61
b. To less-developed countries	8.4	5	35

Source: United Nations, *Monthly Bulletin of Statistics*, November 1968.

The Pattern of World Trade

Recent trends in world trade lend some support to the pessimistic view that trade with the center will not impart sufficient stimulus to the periphery. In Table 6–1 we see that, with world exports totalling $177 billion, developed countries accounted for $141 billion, or 79 per cent. Exports from less-developed to developed countries—the trade flow that must transmit the impulse to growth from center to periphery—amounted to only $29 billion, or 16 per cent of the total. Furthermore, trade among developed countries is growing faster than imports from the less developed. Trade among developed countries grew by 117 per cent from 1957 to 1967, while developed countries' imports from less-developed countries grew by only 61 per cent.

These aggregate trade figures hide some significant differences among the low-income countries. Fully one fourth of all exports from the periphery flow from a handful of petroleum-producing countries, brightening their development prospects. Their oil exports have financed huge payments deficits incurred by the rest of the economy, paying for imports of capital goods and consumer goods. Of more importance for the rest of the less-developed world, trends in exports of manufactured goods, on which many countries base their development prospects, have been adverse to the low-income countries. In Table 6–2 we see that trade in manufactures is even more concentrated among the developed countries than total trade; over 90 per cent originates in the center. Manufactured exports from less-developed countries have been rising sharply, faster than developed countries' exports. But this hopeful statistic needs to be qualified. First, the manu-

103

Table 6–2 TRADE IN MANUFACTURED PRODUCTS* BETWEEN DEVELOPED AND LESS-DEVELOPED COUNTRIES

Trade Flow	Value of Trade in Billions of Dollars		Percentage Increase
	1957	1967	
1. World exports	48.2	110.4	118
2. Exports of developed countries	45.1	102.8	128
a. To developed countries	28.8	79.4	177
b. To less-developed countries	16.3	23.4	44
3. Exports of less developed countries	3.1	7.5	142
a. To developed countries	2.1	5.2	148
b. To less-developed countries	1.0	2.3	130

*All products in the Standard International Trade Classification sections 5–8.
Source: United Nations, *Monthly Bulletin of Statistics,* November 1968.

factured exports of less-developed countries are still very small; the percentage increase reflects this low starting point and is, therefore, somewhat misleading. Second, a very small number of less-developed countries account for the bulk of these manufactured exports; a mere *three* countries (Hong Kong, India, and Yugoslavia) account for 40 per cent, and 14 countries for fully 75 per cent. Finally, these exports are highly concentrated in a narrow range of products— light manufactures, textiles, clothing, footwear, and others—with a high labor content. They often involve raw-materials processing. As we shall see, these exports run into high tariff walls erected by advanced countries. If trade is to provide significant, widespread development impulses, the advanced countries must, through their own policies, open the door wider to imports from the periphery.

The developing countries do not expect primary-product exports to provide growth impulses. Growth prospects here threaten to be sluggish. A U.N. study projects the growth of primary-product imports by developed countries at an annual rate of between 2.4 and 2.8 per cent. The experience of individual countries and commodities will far exceed these projected growth rates, but the overall picture is pessimistic. Many economists also believe that the prices of primary products will follow a declining trend. These prices did fall from the Korean War boom until 1962; however no general trend has been apparent since, but some commodities have suffered further severe price declines.

It has long been believed that the prices of primary products are subject to violent short-term fluctuations. The supply and demand curves of primary products are alleged to be highly unstable. Moreover, low short-run price elasticities of supply and demand are believed to transform a slight shift in either curve into a large price change. This alleged instability of prices is said to cause sharp fluctuations in total export earnings, which force cutbacks in imports and endanger development plans. There is, however, only weak statistical evidence of greater-than-average instability in primary product prices, although some countries have indeed suffered from severe short-term fluctuations in export earnings.

There is also no firm evidence that countries experiencing abnormal instability have, as a consequence, shown slower growth.

Trade Policy in Developing Countries

Economic planners in the less-developed countries have rejected a simple application of comparative advantage. Straightforward application of this principle would cause them to concentrate on exporting traditional primary products and importing manufactured goods. Instead, they wish to industrialize, justifying their choice on twin grounds—the gloomy demand prospect for primary products, and infant-industry and market-imperfection arguments for protection. Many less-developed countries have engaged in extensive *import substitution*. They have sought to industrialize by encouraging the domestic production of previously imported manufactured goods.

This policy at first appears to have great promise. Most governments can look down the list of imported consumer goods, find some that can be manufactured domestically, impose tariffs on the likely prospects, and enjoy an import-substitution boom. At some point, however, the list of unprotected import-competing industries is exhausted, and the homely virtues of comparative advantage are seen in a new light. The economy has been saddled with high-cost industries producing in small, inefficient plants. Because of the limited national market, moreover, industries are dominated by a few firms, with inadequate incentives to introduce modern technology, and unable to export because their costs are above world prices. Further import substitution by capital-goods production is ruled out by the technical complexity and large scale of these industries. This situation, typical of the more advanced Latin American countries, helps to explain the drive to open the markets of the developed world. The experience with import substitution shows again that, although there are legitimate arguments for tariffs, they are easily misapplied, penalizing an economy with inefficient industries.

TRADE POLICY AT THE CENTER

In 1964, the United Nations sponsored its first Conference on Trade and Development (UNCTAD). There, the less-developed countries set forth their goals, problems, and proposals with a clarity, force, and unity that put the developed countries on the defensive. The Final Act of UNCTAD issued a challenge that cannot be ignored:[3]

> Economic development and social progress should be the common concern of the whole international community. . . . Accordingly, all countries pledge

[3]United Nations, *Trade and Development, Final Act and Report,* New York, 1964, p. 10.

themselves to pursue internal and external economic policies designed to accelerate economic growth throughout the world, and in particular to help promote, in developing countries, a rate of growth consistent with the need to bring about a substantial and steady increase in average income. . . .

Four years later, after UNCTAD II, its Secretary-General observed bitterly that "only very limited positive results that are not commensurate with the dimensions and urgency of the development problem" have as yet been achieved.[4]

The challenge of UNCTAD was to adopt new methods for spurring the growth of less-developed countries. If, of course, the center countries manage their own economies to achieve steady growth, the less-developed countries will enjoy a growing demand for their exports. Reassured by domestic prosperity, moreover, the center countries will be more willing to honor their obligations abroad. Furthermore, the balance-of-payments problems of individual center countries do not justify neglect by the center as a whole of the developing countries' need for trade and capital. The center must be "outward-looking" in its trade policies to draw the less-developed countries into the world economy and away from wasteful policies aimed at self-sufficiency.

Yet, our examination of world trade during the recent prosperous past shows that these general policies are only a beginning. Many developing countries, because of sluggish export prospects and heavy debt payments, lack the foreign exchange they need to import capital goods. They also need market incentives to foster production for export. At UNCTAD, therefore, they asked for new policies deliberately to promote exports from the periphery and for a substantial increase in foreign aid to supplement export earnings. Foreign aid is desired for two reasons: it augments domestic capital formation, otherwise limited by low domestic savings, and brings with it the foreign exchange needed to import capital goods.

Commercial Policy

UNCTAD is peculiarly the forum of the less-developed countries—the international economic institution in which they have the dominant voice. Its very existence highlights their disenchantment with the progress made by institutions such as GATT. The GATT principles of reciprocity and nondiscrimination tend to operate in the interests of the center countries. Having the most significant tariff concessions to offer, they are able to obtain the largest tariff cuts on their own exports. As a result, GATT has done little to reduce the obstacles impeding the growth of exports from the less-developed countries.

Primary products are the most prominent target of import controls. Temperate-zone agricultural products compete with domestic production in the United States and Europe, and are heavily restricted, most by quotas and variable levies.

[4]United Nations, *The Significance of the Second Session of the United Nations Conference on Trade and Development*, New York, 1968, p. 1.

These products include wheat, rye, cotton, sugar, and tobacco (the last three being of major importance to many less-developed countries). In addition, tropical products such as bananas, coffee, cocoa, and tea are subjected to heavy excise taxes by some European countries. Although the duties on these products are not protective—Europe does not grow such tropical foods—they are no less damaging to the less-developed countries; by raising the prices paid by consumers, they reduce consumption. Finally, the United States sells its own farm surpluses to less-developed countries on concessionary terms that may hurt competing producers and may even injure the recipient countries. Under the Food for Peace program (Public Law 480), the U.S. government sells surplus wheat and other farm products to low-income countries for their own currencies rather than dollars, allowing those countries to increase their food imports without using up their precious foreign-exchange earnings. The program has been praised for warding off famine in countries with food deficits (especially India), but has also been accused of displacing the food exports of other low-income countries and of causing the recipient countries themselves to rely on U.S. food and thereby to neglect investment in domestic food production. Recent changes in the program have been responsive to these defects. What have often, in practice, been food grants are now outright sales, and food sales are now more closely tied to programs that improve agricultural production in the recipient countries.

Agricultural protectionism need not violate GATT rules; quotas on agricultural products are permitted when a domestic price-support program is in effect. But it violates the spirit of GATT, which frowns on quotas and other nontariff barriers, and lends substance to the UNCTAD view that GATT procedures favor the major industrial powers. In the 1960s, GATT began to respond to these criticisms; it adopted an "Action Program" in 1963 and a new chapter on Trade and Development in 1965. The Action Program called for the prohibition of new trade barriers on products of particular interest to less-developed countries, for the elimination of duties (and internal taxes) on tropical products and of quotas incompatible with GATT on imports from less-developed countries, and for tariff reductions on manufactured exports important to the less-developed countries. The Chapter on Trade and Development also calls for measures to open center country markets and asserts the important principle that developed countries should not expect reciprocity from less-developed countries in the process of reducing trade barriers.

Unhappily, the advanced countries have not responded fully to these recommendations: many have even ignored the Action Program's call for an end to excise taxes on tropical products. In flagrant violation of GATT intentions, moreover, a Long-Term Arrangement for Cotton Textiles has established quotas on cotton textile imports into the industrial nations. This agreement reflected the rapid growth of cotton textile exports from Japan, Hong Kong, and other Asian countries, that had "disrupted" markets in a few importing countries, particularly the United States and the United Kingdom. It antedates the Action Program, and

107

was to be phased out, but was renewed for three more years in 1967. It is deemed to be "voluntary," as the exporting nations agreed to it (under pressure). Hence it does not violate the GATT rule against quotas. Further, it is designed to allow some growth in the restricted exports. But it makes a mockery of the center countries' promises, and has ominous implications for the future. The United States has suggested a similar agreement for other textiles, implying that whenever a low-income country successfully penetrates a center country's market, protectionist presssures will force the erection of new trade barriers. The low-income country's investment in export production will be wasted time after time.

A policy to stimulate exports from the periphery clearly must combat such quantitative limitations. The recent GATT agreements, however, call for positive measures too, especially reductions in tariffs on goods important to the less-developed countries. Center country tariffs on these manufactured goods are still rather high, averaging around 12 per cent, but with much higher rates on some items. These goods are labor-intensive products, like textiles and clothing, in which the labor-abundant less-developed countries have a comparative advantage. Because of their labor-intensity and simple technology, output per man-hour does not differ very much from country to country. A garment worker at a sewing machine is just as efficient in Hong Kong or Bombay as in New York or Milan, giving the low-wage countries a distinct cost advantage. These industries, however, have had difficulties in the high-wage industrial countries, preceding the growth of output in the less-developed countries, and respond to additional imports with cries for protection. Unfortunately, the American government responded to their cries by negotiating import quotas on cotton textiles, rather than by providing adjustment assistance to move resources out of the industry.

Against this background, it is not surprising that the Kennedy Round, a great success for trade among the center countries, was a relative failure from the point of view of the periphery, with average tariffs on their exports falling less than those on center country exports. Although tariffs on some of their manufactures were reduced significantly—on leather goods, footwear, and some processed foodstuffs—many tariffs stayed high. In addition, tariff reductions on other products, such as cotton textiles, will not increase trade because it is restricted by quotas.

Tariff Preferences

Although the center countries have evinced little interest in tariff reductions on products important to the low-income countries, the less-developed countries continue to press for reductions. They seek, indeed, to go further and receive tariff *preferences* on their manufactured exports. A preferential reduction in tariffs would breach the first principle of GATT, the doctrine of nondiscrimination embodied in the most-favored-nation clause. The exports of the less-developed countries would enter center countries duty-free or at lower duties than the comparable exports of other developed countries.

Some have argued that preferences cannot much increase the exports of less-developed countries. Suppose that the Japanese are the cheapest developed-country exporters of clothing goods. If an Indian manufacturer can export clothing to the United States more cheaply than a Japanese, preferential treatment is unnecessary; nondiscriminatory tariff reduction is the most that is needed. For a preference to help, the Indian's export price must be higher than that of his Japanese competitor, but lower than the American domestic price. The U.S. domestic price will equal the Japanese price (the cheapest world price) plus the U.S. tariff. If the Indian's price is higher than the Japanese but lower than the American, a preferential tariff cut could be designed to give the Indian producer access to the U.S. market (at the expense of the Japanese). If tariff rates are low, however, the range between the Japanese and American prices will be quite narrow. Hence, few producers in the less-developed countries would benefit from preferences.

But many tariff rates are high, even after the Kennedy Round and especially on labor-intensive manufactures, giving preferences much room to operate. These *nominal* tariff rates, moreover, do not fully measure their restrictive effect or the scope for preferences. We have instead to look at *effective tariffs*. Suppose raw cotton bears no import duty, but cotton shirts are taxed at 20 per cent. The effective protection afforded cotton-shirt manufacturing is much higher than 20 per cent. If raw cotton accounts for half the final price of shirts, the other half being *value added* by the shirt manufacturer, the American manufacturer benefits from a 40 per cent *effective tariff*. The 20 per cent levied on the *full price* of the shirt is protection afforded the value added by the manufacturer, and this is only half the full price of the shirt. The *effective* rate is the proceeds of the nominal rate divided by the value that is added in the activity being protected. To illustrate with particular numbers, suppose that the raw cotton costs $3 and the pretariff import price is $6. A 20 per cent tariff levied on $6 yields $1.20 in duties. Dividing by the $3.00 of value added in shirt manufacturing, we obtain a 40 per cent effective rate for the manufacturing activity. If any raw materials used by an activity are subject to duty, the effective rate is reduced, but the effective rate will be higher than the nominal rate as long as the nominal rate on the output in question is higher than the average duty on the inputs used.[5]

Nominal tariffs tend typically to *escalate* by stage of production; they are lowest on raw materials and increase with the amount of processing. This tariff structure causes effective rates to be higher than nominal rates, since the duty on inputs will generally be lower than those on finished goods. Table 6-3 compares effective and nominal rates. The effective rates are substantially higher. Nominal and effective rates tend also to be higher on consumer goods than capital goods. Hence, effective protection is greatest on the goods most important to the less-

---

[5]The precise formula for the rate of effective protection is the nominal tariff rate *minus* the average nominal tariff rate on material inputs (weighted by their contribution to the cost of the output) divided by the fraction of value added contributed by the protected activity.

developed countries—processed raw materials and consumer goods. Table 6-3 shows that both nominal and effective protection is greater on the exports of less-developed countries than on manufactured goods in general. Table 6-3 also shows that the Kennedy Round cut tariffs more for developed countries than for low-income countries. Tariffs on the manufactured exports of the less-developed countries are still significant.

Table 6–3 NOMINAL AND EFFECTIVE TARIFFS ON MANUFACTURED PRODUCTS (percentages)

	Total Imports of Manufactures		Imports of Manufactures from Developing Countries	
	Nominal	Effective	Nominal	Effective
United States				
Pre-Kennedy Round	11.5	20.0	17.9	35.4
Post-Kennedy Round	6.8	11.6	12.4	23.9
European Economic Community				
Pre-Kennedy Round	11.0	18.6	14.3	27.7
Post-Kennedy Round	6.6	11.1	9.4	16.9

Source: B. Balassa, "The Structure of Protection in Industrial Countries and its Effects on the Exports of Processed Goods from Developing Countries," in UNCTAD, *The Kennedy Round Estimated Effects on Tariff Barriers*, 1968.

Preferences granted on nominal tariffs will create larger effective preferences. If the Indian shirt exporter received a 50 per cent preference (his goods being charged a 10 per cent duty), effective protection would fall from 40 per cent to 20 per cent ($.60/3.00) giving him a 20 percentage point advantage over a Japanese exporter. If Indian exports entered duty-free, the effective preference would be 40 percentage points. Clearly, preferences may significantly increase the less-developed countries' exports to the industrial center.

But preferences are still enmeshed in controversy. Proponents cite the Kennedy Round as proof that GATT methods will not help the low-income countries; a more deliberate policy is needed. They also invoke a version of the infant-industry and economies-of-scale arguments: producers in low-income countries need favored treatment before they can compete on equal terms in advanced country markets.[6] Proponents add that preferences will lure foreign investors into less-developed countries, to profit from preferential treatment on exports to other advanced countries. Finally, they say, preferences will cost the advanced countries very little.

Opponents of preferences predict an enormous increase in the complexity of

[6]This use of the infant-industry argument is inexact. With preferential tariff treatment, consumers in the advanced countries subsidize producers in the low-income countries. In the infant-industry case, consumers in the low-income country supply the subsidy (by paying higher prices). A preference is, in a sense, a concealed resource transfer and an inefficient form of foreign aid. But this does not constitute a sufficient argument against preferences; it may be politically advantageous (for both donor and recipient) to give aid in this fashion.

customs administration, and are worried by the inequitable and inefficient way in which the benefits might be distributed, and the political dependence they are likely to create between the giver and receiver of preferences. When we consider specific schemes, the force of some of these objections will be clearer, but we should remember that complexity invites ingenuity, not outright rejection.

Although the United States stood alone against preferences at UNCTAD I, it has since joined the other developed countries, accepting the principle. But unanimity exists only in principle, and many competing preference schemes flourish. Two basic issues separate the many plans. First, as less-developed countries differ in their capacity to exploit preferences, uniform preference margins sufficient to aid semi-industrial countries would barely help the more backward countries. This issue can be resolved only by giving wide preference margins or by providing special treatment to the least-developed countries. Secondly, as advanced countries differ in their vulnerability to an increase in exports from the less-developed countries and in tariff levels, uniform preferences on all imports would affect them differently. Most schemes thus have "safeguards" built into them—exclusions of either specific products or of a specific country's exports of those products (e.g., Hong Kong's cotton textiles), or quotas and escape clauses to be invoked if preferential exports create unacceptable "disruption."

The UNCTAD preference plan calls for duty-free preferential access for *all* less-developed countries and for all semimanufactures and manufactures, without restriction on quantity. Safeguard provisions would be permitted in specific cases, and preferences would be limited in duration, with ten years given as an initial figure. UNCTAD also suggests that special attention be given to the needs of the "less-advanced developing countries" (by way of longer preferences or an exclusion from safeguard provisions). Countries that would lose existing preferential treatment in advanced country markets would receive equivalent new preferences.

The present preferential arrangements of the EEC and British Commonwealth raise the most divisive issues in the discussions among the advanced countries. Imports from the former colonies of EEC members and of the United Kingdom already receive favored treatment, while EEC and British exports receive "reverse preferences" in these less-developed countries. The United States opposes these special preferential groupings and "reverse preferences," favoring uniform nondiscriminatory preferences. We fear the division of the world into trading blocs, with the Europeans giving preferences to Asian and African countries and the United States giving preferences to Latin America. The Europeans seem willing to reduce discriminatory preference margins if equivalent concessions are given to the less-developed countries losing their privilged positions. But some, especially France, are unwilling to part with "reverse preferences."

Policies for Primary Products

The less-developed countries have sought several ways to curb the instability of raw-material prices or to obtain compensatory aid. Although the extent of price fluctuations and their adverse consequences have probably been exagger-   **111** ated, reduced fluctuations in export earnings will help countries whose development plans are threatened by possible export shortfalls.

Commodity agreements, however, have not been too successful. The International Sugar Agreement imposed export quotas on producing countries in order to regulate supply; the International Tin Agreement set up a *buffer stock* of tin under the management of a Council and instructed the Council to buy and sell tin so as to smooth out prices. Another agreement covering coffee also uses export quotas, but tries as well to regulate production by encouraging coffee producers to diversify their crops. Each of these agreements has encountered problems. It is difficult to penalize countries that exceed their export quotas, driving sugar prices down. It is difficult to know which movements in tin prices should be offset by transactions involving the buffer stock. (At one point, incidentally, the Tin Council ran out of tin and could not keep the price down; in fact, prices soared on word that the stock was low). Countries that exceed their coffee export quotas try to get larger quotas rather than cut production. And all of these agreements have one major flaw: although working to dampen short-term fluctuations, they also tend to freeze commodity prices, suppressing vital signals of long-run change in world supply and demand. They thereby distort resource allocation, much as the American price-support program tends to keep too much labor in agriculture. Moreover, the agreements that rely on quotas tend also to freeze world production patterns, preventing the small but efficient producer from increasing its share of the market.

For all these reasons, governments are looking for new approaches to stabilization—for ways of compensating low-income countries when their export earnings fall, rather than for ways of manipulating market prices. One such plan is already in operation: In 1963, the International Monetary Fund offered supplementary drawing rights to countries whose export earnings drop below trend. IMF drawings, however, must be repaid within a few years; they are short-term aid and cannot be used to offset a "persistent" short-fall in export earnings. Partly for this reason the supplementary drawing rights have been used sparingly, India making the largest drawing—$90 million in 1967. Another, more ambitious plan, would offer sufficient aid to prevent disruption of development programs. Drafted by the International Bank for Reconstruction and Development, the plan would establish a new agency able to assist a country when its export earnings fell below an agreed-upon projected level; the country could meet the foreign-exchange needs of its development program unhampered by balance-of-payments crises. The scheme, which is still under study, also contains liberal long-term repayment provisions.

Some economists have expressed scepticism about the need for such plans. They doubt that fluctuations in export prices are the cause of the balance-of-payments troubles of less-developed countries, pointing instead to internal policies that cause the supply of exports to fall or the demand for imports to rise beyond development needs. They add, quite rightly, that the most urgent and fundamental need is improved access to center country markets—dismantling agricultural protectionism in the United States and Europe.

THE FLOW OF CAPITAL

If the less-developed countries could count on steadily expanding export opportunities, their development prospects would be enhanced. Nevertheless, to achieve even modest rates of economic growth, they need more foreign exchange and capital than exports and domestic saving can provide. In 1968, over $11 billion of official and private capital flowed from the center countries to the less-developed countries. Table 6–4 shows that foreign aid accounted for $7 billion of this total. Yet, large as this seems, it is thought by many to be inadequate.[7]

Table 6–4 FLOW OF CAPITAL TO THE LESS-DEVELOPED COUNTRIES AND MULTILATERAL DEVELOPMENT ORGANIZATIONS, 1968

(billions of dollars)

Type of Capital and Source	Amount
Official Capital	$ 7.1
United States	3.6
Bilateral	3.3
Grants and grant-like contributions	1.7
Government long-term capital (net)	1.6
Multilateral	0.3
Other Developed Countries*	3.5
Bilateral	3.1
Grants and grant-like contributions	1.7
Government long-term capital (net)	1.4
Multilateral	0.4
Private Capital	4.2
United States	2.2
Direct investment**	1.6
Portfolio investment and other (net)***	0.6
Other Developed Countries	2.0
Direct investment****	1.3
Portfolio investment and other (net)***	0.7
Total—Official and Private	11.3

*The other members of the Development Assistance Committee.
**Includes $480 million of reinvested earnings.
***Includes private purchases of IBRD bonds; excludes private export credits.
****Includes reinvested earnings.
Source: Organization for Economic Co-operation and Development, *Development Assistance, 1969 Review.*

[7]These figures are for the 16 nations constituting the Development Assistance Committee of the OECD; they contribute the overwhelming bulk of aid to the less-developed countries. When aid flows are given, DAC figures are meant.

The less-developed countries could make efficient use of much larger amounts. The donors, moreover, could afford much more. Aid now represents only 0.4 of 1 per cent of the donors' GNP. The United States is by far the largest single contributor, but it ranks eighth out of 16 countries in the percentage of its national income transferred through foreign aid.

To make matters worse, U.S. economic aid has fallen off sharply in recent years. The United States has been giving aid for a quarter-century: economic aid to Europe under the Marshall Plan, military and economic assistance to political allies, and in the last decade, substantial amounts of aid to spur economic development—directly through the Agency for International Development (AID), and indirectly through international organizations. Many Americans, viewing the continued poverty of the less-developed countries, are discouraged by the apparent failure of development aid. Sharing this view, Congress has slashed progressively smaller aid requests coming from the White House, appropriating only $1.3 billion in 1969.[8] Foreign aid now seems to be merely a holding operation.

Too much was expected of economic aid. Development depends primarily upon the recipients' own efforts. External assistance can supplement a serious development effort, but it cannot guarantee economic growth in a country that lacks the political and economic prerequisites or mismanages its own economic affairs. One has also to remember that many less-developed countries have in fact achieved high growth rates: since 1960, more than 40 countries have grown faster than 4 per cent per annum, and 20 countries faster than 6 per cent. But poverty is still so pervasive that the public in donor countries cannot perceive progress, and they come to believe that aid funds are being wasted.

The reaction against aid-giving has come at a dangerous time, for many less-developed countries are now endangered by sharply rising foreign indebtedness. The total public foreign debt of developing countries was $47 billion in mid-1968,[9] and service payments on this debt (interest plus repayment of principal) exceeded $4 billion. Some countries' debt-service payments use up more than 20 per cent of their total export earnings. Some have been forced to seek relief by an agreed postponement of repayment; Argentina, Brazil, Chile, Ghana, Indonesia, and India have recently renegotiated their external liabilities. The levels of both debt and service payments have grown at rates higher than 10 per cent per year for most countries and higher than 20 per cent for many. From 1956 to 1967, India's debt grew at 25 per cent and Pakistan's grew at 32 per cent. These rates far exceed the growth of output and have far different implications than growth in internal public debt. The rapid build-up in debt reflects the large recent capital flows to the low-income countries, and, as we can see in Table 6-4, the large role of loans in the total.

It might seem strange to call an official loan foreign "aid." But government loans are often made on "soft" terms, with long maturities, initial grace periods,

[8]This excludes food aid under Public Law 480.
[9]Estimated by the IBRD for 79 countries.

and interest rates below the market rate. The degree of "aid" (or "grant-element") is less than the face value of the loan and should be measured by the loan's "softness." AID loans began as very soft loans (at ¾ of 1 per cent interest), but Congress has progressively hardened the terms (to 3 per cent). Hardening not only reduces the degree of aid involved but stores up more serious debt-service problems for the borrowers. One close student of foreign aid has warned that:[10]

> . . . if terms of development loans cannot be softened drastically and universally, and this does not at present seem very likely, then one must probably look forward to an era of consolidation exercises, threats of default and eventually increasingly insistent demands for moratoria . . . probably the time is not far away when a concerted effort has to be made to put development assistance not merely on a soft, but on a grant basis.

The value of aid can also be reduced by the practice of *tying* aid funds to the purchase of the donor country's products. The United States began tying aid in 1960, and nearly all its aid is now tied to U.S. exports. The purpose of tying is to reduce the balance-of-payments cost of the foreign-aid program by matching aid outflows with exports of American goods. This aim is understandable, but it reduces the value of aid to the recipient government. Aid funds should be used to buy from the cheapest source. The effects of tying would, of course, be minimal if the recipient country can use aid funds to purchase American goods it had already intended to import using export earnings, then use its export earnings to buy other imports. Opportunities for "switching" imports are limited, however, if total planned imports from the United States are less than the amount of tied aid. Moreover, much aid is tied to specific projects and commodities, further reducing opportunities for "switching." According to various estimates, tying raises average import costs by as much as 20 per cent, and 100 per cent price differentials between tied and untied sources have been reported.

Difficulties with bilateral aid have stirred a new interest in multilateral aid. Even now, this form of aid is not insignificant. In 1967, multilateral organizations supplied developing countries with about $1.0 billion. The oldest and largest multilateral organization is the IBRD (or World Bank), which floats its own bonds in developed countries' capital markets and makes loans to governments and private firms in the less-developed countries. In 1968–69, the Bank raised $1.2 billion in the United States and Europe and loaned $1.4 billion. It is currently engaged in a plan to double its annual lending to about $1.6 billion, to offset the fall in bilateral aid. It is seeking new sources of capital (borrowing, for example, from "less-developed" countries like Kuwait). There are limits, however, to what the Bank and its various regional counterparts can do.[11] It must pay interest on

[10]Goran Ohlin, *Aid and Indebtedness*, (Paris, 1966), pp. 38–39.
[11]Inter-American Development Bank, the European Investment Bank, and the Asian Development Bank.

its own bonds and has therefore to charge the less-developed countries rates as high as 6½ per cent, intensifying their debt-service problems. The Bank does have a soft-loan subsidiary, the International Development Association (IDA), which lends for 50 years at ¾ of 1 per cent interest. But IDA is completely dependent on contributions from the developed countries. There is a second subsidiary, the International Finance Corporation (IFC) which invests in private enterprises in less-developed countries, and tries to bring in other private capital, acting as a catalyst. But IFC investments have averaged under $70 million in the period 1966–69.

Private Capital

Some economists argue that less-developed countries should be able to attract more private capital. They point to the enormous private capital flows from Europe that went to the periphery in the nineteenth century, developing mines and plantations and financing transportation and public utilities. These economists criticize the low-income countries for relying so heavily on official funds.

Unfortunately there are several flaws in the analogy between the less-developed countries of the nineteenth century and those of the twentieth. To begin with, most nineteenth-century capital transfers were portfolio investments (bond issues) rather than direct investments (the building of factories and other facilities by foreign companies). In addition, investors today are chary of investments in those less-developed countries that have chronic payments problems, maintain exchange control, or have already borrowed hugely, incurring heavy debt-service burdens.

Even in the nineteenth century, moreover, little foreign capital went into manufacturing—yet that is where the less-developed countries want it channeled now. Like many European countries, they have placed their public utilities and transportation systems under state ownership or close regulation.

Finally, the slow growth of demand for raw materials has deterred American companies from expanding their interests in mining and agriculture in the less-developed countries. For that matter, many of those countries are not anxious to attract foreign capital into extractive industries; they equate extraction with exploitation, and want to reduce their dependence on exports of raw materials.

Despite these obstacles, there has been a fair amount of foreign investment in the periphery. Table 6–4 shows that, in 1968, more than $4 billion of private capital flowed to less-developed countries. Direct investment accounted for $2.9 billion of the total.

There are ways to stimulate the flow of private capital. For some time, the United States has provided guaranties against the special hazards of foreign investment—expropriation, exchange depreciation, and war damage. Now, it offers "all risk" guaranties. A company that plans to build a plant abroad can buy a guaranty from the U.S. government, to compensate the company if its assets are confiscated, frozen, or destroyed. Several countries give tax incentives to their investors. The United States, for example, permits an American company to defer its U.S. taxes on income earned and reinvested abroad. German companies can take a temporary tax deduction when they make a new investment overseas.

But mutual wariness between potential investors and the host countries is bound to limit total direct investment. Although many low-income countries welcome foreign capital, and even try to attract it with tax incentives and other favors, many also fear exploitation. Investments, moreover, are expected to contribute strongly to development, unlike the "enclave" investments of the past which, it is felt, brought little benefit. Investors are asked to train resident labor, give management positions to residents, use local resources, and solicit local equity participation. Investors sometimes chafe at these requirements, and resent the ambivalent attitude of many countries towards private investment. They are frequently reluctant to invest in what they term a hostile investment "climate."

Various proposals have been made to break this impasse. These seek to attract the technology and management capabilities of foreign corporations, but to give the host countries partial or complete ownership of the enterprise. In joint ventures, the foreign investor shares ownership with local capitalists. Under management contracts, the foreign company runs the enterprise for a fee, without owning it. Finally, it has been proposed that foreign aid supply the capital for firms, to be owned by the host country, and that foreign corporations supply the management.

All these proposals are worthwhile, but many experts are agreed that the developed countries must show more willingness to give outright aid if we are ever to bridge the gap between rich and poor.

Prospect

Progress in human affairs may sometimes occur by the slow accretion of small changes in existing institutions and arrangements, rather than by radical reform. But if the United States and the other industrial countries are to meet the challenge posed by the new nations, they must draw bolder plans and commit a larger part of their vast resources. Nothing we can do will guarantee success. Trade and aid do not assure development, and development does not assure political stability. It may, in fact, usher in a gigantic upheaval in the new nations. But failure to provide opportunities for trade and to furnish much more aid will certainly inhibit growth at the periphery. Stagnation, moreover, will generate frustrations and discontent that can only bring worse sorts of disorder. To strengthen the industrial center and knit together center and periphery may be the most important and difficult tasks to face the United States at the start of the last quarter of the twentieth century.

Selected Readings

Allen, William R., *International Trade Theory: Hume to Ohlin*. (New York: Random House, 1965.) Excerpts from the classics on trade theory, including the chief contributions of Smith, Ricardo, Mill, and Ohlin.

American Economic Association, *Readings in the Theory of International Trade* (Philadelphia: Blakiston, 1949) and *Readings in International Economics* (Homewood, Illinois: Richard D. Irwin, 1968.) These two volumes contain many of the major contributions to modern trade theory.

Cooper, Richard, *The Economics of Interdependence*. (New York: McGraw-Hill 1968.) International financial policy in a world of highly interdependent national economies.

Condliffe, J.B., *The Commerce of Nations*. (New York: W.W. Norton, 1950.) A detailed history of the international economy, stressing the strategic role of Great Britain.

Friedman, Milton, *Essays in Positive Economics*. (Chicago: University of Chicago Press, 1953.) Contains the classic case for flexible exchange rates.

Haberler, Gottfried, *A Survey of International Trade Theory*, and Corden, W.M., *Recent Developments in the Theory of International Trade*. (Princeton: International Finance Section, 1961 and 1965.) Taken together, these two monographs furnish a comprehensive view of modern theory, shorn of mathematics and complicated diagrams.

Hawkins, R.G., and S.E. Rolfe, *A Critical Survey of Plans for International Monetary Reform*. (New York: C.J. Devine Institute, New York University, 1965.) A description and comparison of the best-known plans.

Hicks, J.R., *Essays in World Economics*. (London: Oxford University Press, 1959.) Chapter 3 is a brilliant restatement of the case for free trade.

Johnson, Harry G., *Economic Policies Toward Less Developed Countries*. (Washington, D.C.: The Brookings Institution, 1967.) A rigorous review of the major issues in trade and development including treatment of tariff preferences and commodity agreements.

118

Krause, Lawrence B., *European Economic Integration and the United States*. (Washington, D.C.: The Brookings Institution, 1968.) Contains an extensive attempt to measure the impact of the EEC and EFTA on U.S. trade.

Machlup, Fritz, *Remaking the International Monetary System: The Rio Agreement and Beyond.* (Baltimore: Johns Hopkins, 1968.) A detailed discussion of Special Drawing Rights.

Meade, James E., *The Balance of Payments.* (London: Oxford University Press, 1951.) The classic treatise on balance-of-payments adjustment under various exchange-rate regimes.

Mikesell, Raymond F., *Public International Lending for Development.* (New York: Random House, 1966.) A compact survey of the major aid programs and institutions, raising and reviewing the problems that lie ahead.

Nurkse, Ragnar, *International Currency Experience.* (Geneva: League of Nations, 1944.) A description and critique of international monetary policies during the inter-war period—which exerted tremendous influence on postwar planning.

————, *Equilibrium and Growth in the World Economy.* (Cambridge: Harvard University Press, 1961.) Our treatment of "center and periphery" owes much to Nurkse's view; see especially Chapters 7 and 11.

Pincus, John, *Trade, Aid and Development: The Rich and Poor Nations.* (New York: McGraw-Hill, 1967.) A very useful discussion of trade and foreign aid issues.

Prebisch, Raul, *Towards a New Trade Policy for Development.* (New York: United Nations, 1964.) The Secretary General of UNCTAD reviews the roles of trade and aid in fostering development; an influential and controversial document.

Robinson, Joan, "The Pure Theory of International Trade," *Review of Economic Studies,* Vol. XIV, No. 2 (1946/47). A superb synthesis of trade theories, with special attention to the role of wages.

Tsiang, S.C., "Fluctuating Exchange Rates in Countries with Relatively Stable Economies," *International Monetary Fund Staff Papers,* Vol. VII, No. 2 (October, 1959). An interesting contrast with Nurkse's critical reading of inter-war experience.